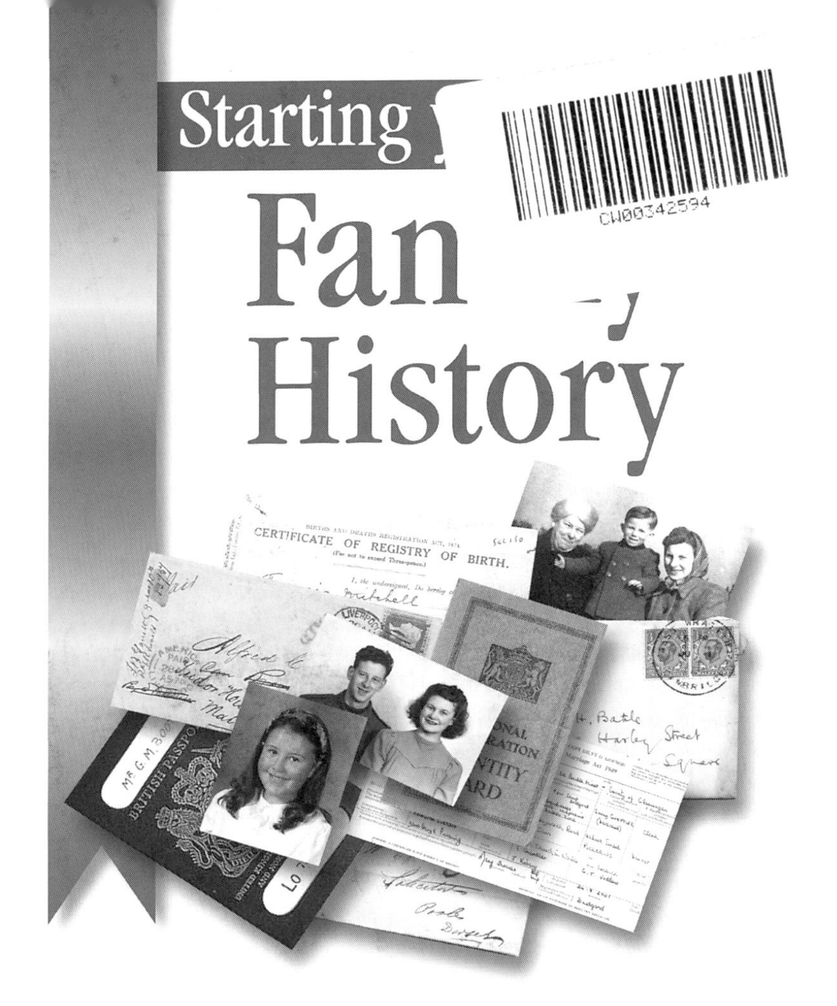

Margaret Ward

With a Foreword by John Titford

COUNTRYSIDE BOOKS
NEWBURY BERKSHIRE

First published 2006

Reprinted 2007

COUNTRYSIDE BOOKS
3 Catherine Road
Newbury, Berkshire

To view our complete range of books,
please visit us at
www.countrysidebooks.co.uk

ISBN 1 85306 885 3
EAN 978 1 85306 885 0

Designed by Peter Davies, Nautilus Design
Produced through MRM Associates Ltd., Reading
Printed by Cambridge University Press

Contents

Foreword

Carrying out family history research is rather like running a London marathon. You do it because it's fun and it's a challenge; everyone is welcome, regardless of their level of ability and experience; there's no hurry and it's the taking part that counts.

If you're a raw beginner, you can expect a warm welcome in the world of family history. Others who can remember the days when they, too, were just starting out will be only too pleased to help in whatever way they can. You can join a family history society, subscribe to a family history magazine and chat to those whose experience means that they know their way around better than you do.

Above all, you can read Margaret Ward's book, *Starting Your Family History*. She makes it clear that research of this kind involves a process, a progression, as you work your way steadily through relevant material, from that most fundamental of primary sources - your own family: through names, dates and much else, until you really feel you can recreate the lives of your ancestors.

Margaret Ward has been there, has done it. Let her be the friend at your side, encouraging, informing - warning you of potential pitfalls, even - as she guides you in an uncomplicated way through a series of journeys into the past that will feel at times almost like your very own ancestral soap opera.

So, why not get started on an increasingly popular pastime which will intrigue you for years to come? It's time to activate those 'little grey cells' ...

Enjoy!

John Titford

Introduction

Finding out who we are and where our roots are is a desire that is common to people from all walks of life and of all ages. Something acts on us to spark off that interest - a television programme, perhaps, or finding an old family photograph or a set of war medals - and before we know it, we are 'family historians', and absorbed by a hobby that will perhaps become a lifelong passion.

You may simply want to find out who your grandparents were, perhaps even your parents. Or you may want to carry on working back through time as far as you can, and to trace as many families as possible who contributed to making you what you are. The choice is yours - this is your family history, after all. You do not have to have a computer, either, though it is a very useful tool and the Internet will certainly help you to locate records from the comfort of your own home.

This is a book for beginners, which starts with your best source - yourself and your family - and then introduces the main records to consult in order to create your family tree, such as certificates of births, marriages and deaths, census returns, parish registers and wills. Chapters on the records of the poor, nonconformists, military ancestors, and suggestions for what to look for outside the archives, give an idea of the wide range of sources available. Discover, for instance, where your ancestors went to school, what they did for a living, how they voted, where they lived and what they did in the war.

Family history can be a satisfying solitary hobby or it can be a means to making friends all over the world. Sometimes people prefer to work on their own, enjoying the challenge of solving problems and tracking down ancestors who seem determined not to be found. But, join a family history society or an Internet mailing list, and you quickly find that there are many others out there with similar interests to your own, who are willing to share their knowledge and help you if they can. Some of them may turn out to be part of your extended family!

Margaret Ward

Chapter 1

How Do I Start?

When you begin to trace the history of a family it is easy to overlook the familiar in the excitement of the chase. It is wise counsel that advises starting with what you know and working back through the generations, step by step. Today, with so many tempting goodies available at the touch of a button on the Internet, it is easy to forget that there are very good reasons for taking the time to see that the roots of your family tree are firmly planted.

Every time you add a name or generation to your family history, you must be sure that you have proved the link beyond doubt. Why make mistakes now that will dog you for years and may even send you in the wrong direction entirely, or that will make other family historians doubt your reliability? So, even if you have already dipped into the archives here and there, just for a moment put that all to one side and focus on your primary source – you and your family.

Start with yourself

Most people will be able to come up with enough information for a rough and ready family tree going back approximately 100 years – yourself, plus your parents and then your grandparents, as each generation is reckoned to cover about 30 years. If you have children, grandchildren, or even great-grandchildren, including their names and details (dates of birth, dates of marriage and so on) will also bring the tree forward and lay the foundations for the future.

Simply answer the following questions, as fully as you are able:

1. Your full first names
2. Your date and place of birth
3. The name of your spouse, and the date and place of your marriage

4. The names and details of your children, and their children
5. The names and details of your brothers and sisters
6. Your father's and mother's full names (including your mother's maiden name)
7. Their dates and places of birth
8. The date and place of their marriage
9. The dates of their deaths and places of burial, if applicable
10. The names and details of their brothers and sisters (your aunts and uncles)
11. For each of your four grandparents, their full names
12. Their dates and places of birth
13. The dates and places of their marriages
14. The dates of their deaths and places of burial, if applicable
15. The names and details of any of their brothers and sisters you remember (your great-uncles and great-aunts)

You may not know, for instance, the actual dates of your grandparents' births, or marriages, but perhaps you can remember when their birthdays fell, or where they lived when you were a child. You may only know their 'family' names (which surprisingly often bear no relation to the name they were actually baptised with!) but it is all useful information. Just write down any small detail you can think of, as it could be an invaluable clue when you begin to research in earnest. Add the occupations your family have followed, too.

All this information will have to be checked and verified by comparison with the records that are discussed in the following chapters. But you now have the beginnings of your family tree in front of you.

Talk to your family

Now you can begin to fill in the gaps by gathering information from the rest of the family, enlisting their help and interest.

Photographs form an important part of the family archive but so often there is no indication as to whom the people are. Unusually, this photograph is not only located to Bromley, Kent, by the photographer's advertisement on the back, but there is also a pencilled note: 'Mary and Nancy Anderson'. (Author's collection)

copies from the General Register Office. Look out, too, for newspaper clippings such as birth notices or obituaries; baptismal cards; wedding ephemera; 'in memoriam' cards or papers relating to a funeral; copies of wills; and so on.

2. Photographs

Nothing is quite so exciting as finding an actual likeness of an ancestor. Ask everyone in the family what photographs they may have lying around.

3. Diaries, letters, cards etc.

Old letters, diaries, holiday postcards, Christmas or birthday cards, address books or birthday books could all be of interest.

4. School records

School reports are often unintentionally funny and might reveal new sides to a well-known character, such as when you discover your taciturn father was once a naughty child 'inclined to chatter'. The dates of the reports will tie up with ages, and the location of the school could help you track down a family address; mention of absences may indicate childhood illnesses. Books, inscribed on the flyleaf, may have been given as prizes for attendance or good work.

5. Other papers

There could be, for instance, certificates for achievements such as lifesaving or ballroom dancing; old passports; papers relating to work such as contracts of employment; a family bible in which some helpful person has written a list of family births.

6. Wartime bits and pieces

Not only papers and photographs, but actual souvenirs such as shell cases made into ashtrays may jog a memory or two. Finding medals can be a real bonus.

There really is no end to the number of family papers and possessions that may help you to fill in your family's background by confirming dates, ages, addresses and relationships, and that are precious connections with the past. When you have identified them, you may want to consider how best you can preserve them for future generations to handle and enjoy.

Finding out more

Basic Approach to Making Contact with Relatives, Peter C. Amsden, FFHS, 1999

Basic Facts About Sources for Family History in the Home, Iain Swinnerton, FFHS, 1996

Basic Facts About Descendant Tracing, Tom Wood, FFHS, 2002

Dating 19th Century Photographs, Robert Pols, FFHS, 2005

Dating 20th Century Photographs, Robert Pols, FFHS, 2005

Chapter 2

Preparing for Action

It is a good idea at this stage to identify your aims. You will have already realised that it is very easy to become overwhelmed by information and possibilities.

Who do you want to research?

There is no hard and fast rule that you must do your research in a certain way. Each time you go back a generation you double the number of possible families you can incorporate into your tree: with your grandparents you have four surnames to trace, your great-grandparents add another four, and by the time you get to your great-great-grandparents, you have sixteen names on your list. Filling in the Birth Brief shown on page 15 is a good way of seeing the situation at a glance.

Most people trace their father's line, since that is the one that has given them their surname. This has the advantage of concentrating your energies on one name, tracing it as far back as you are able.

However, there are other options:

1. You could take the family lines of each of your grandparents, giving you four surnames to work on. (Adding in every wife's surname as you go back will expand it even further.) This can become unwieldy, but it does have the advantage that if you get stuck on one line, there are plenty of other ancestors to go on with.
2. It is possible to do a one-name study, drawing in every reference to a particular surname that can be found, even if the person concerned is not actually part of your family tree.
3. You could research your direct female line (i.e. your mother's mother, her mother and so on). It may not be easy, as the surname will change with every generation, but it would be rewarding.
4. Or, if one branch of your ancestors came from a particular village or

area, you might decide to concentrate on them. You could find that you are related to everyone in the village!

5. There is also no reason why, if you have an interest in one family member, you should not simply concentrate on him or her and set their life into its historical context. Perhaps you have a grandfather who fought in the First World War, for example. Family history is still the same whether it has a focus of one, or a cast of dozens.

Has anyone already done it?

Before you do too much work, it will be worth checking to see if your family tree, or part of it, has already been traced. Genealogy is by no means a new pursuit and families with wealth or land have, for centuries, been keen to establish their family trees. Today, the Internet has enabled people all over the world to publish and share their family histories.

- You can find out what is available by investigating published and unpublished family histories and genealogies. Published genealogies have been listed in *The Genealogist's Guide,* G.W. Marshall (1903), *A Genealogical Guide*, J. B. Whitmore (1953) and *The Genealogist's Guide*, G. B. Barrow (1977), while the Society of Genealogists holds a large number of published and unpublished family histories and family trees.

  Look in major libraries and record offices for county histories (Victorian ones usually have extensive genealogies of important families); the *Victoria County History* volumes for your county; published and unpublished biographies and autobiographies; *Heralds' Visitations* from the 16th century onwards; and so on. Knowledgeable library staff will be of immense help here. The Federation of Family History Societies has published a series of Genealogical Bibliographies by Stuart Raymond.

- On the Internet, simply putting a name into a good search engine will bring up hundreds, if not many thousands of hits, which may or may not be of interest. It does help if you have an unusual surname! There are many web pages, too, set up by family historians happy to share their researches and you should certainly investigate this source.

interests. Members are also always willing to share advice on research and information about computer software and programs.

- *Family Tree Magazine* has a 'contact' column for readers. There is also the *Genealogical Research Directory*, available as a book or CD-ROM, in which you can advertise your surname interests, for a fee; see their website www.ozemail.com.au/~grdxxx (e-mail grdxxx@ozemail.com.au) or write to their British agent: Mrs Elizabeth Simpson, 104 Repton Road, West Bridgford, Notts NG2 7EL.
- On the Web, join a mailing list or newsgroup. This lets you find out what other people with your interests are doing and you can ask questions and for advice. There are many such genealogical discussion groups, some based around a place such as a particular county, others with special interests such as canal people or watchmakers. For more information, visit www.rootsweb.com or www.british-genealogy.com/lists/all-lists.html.
- There are courses for family history beginners run all over the country, by local colleges or bodies such as the Workers Educational Association or the University of the Third Age. Your local library should be able to find out what is going on in your area.
- If you live far from your ancestral home, or your time is limited, there are professional researchers who will undertake work for you for a fee. Many advertise in the columns of the genealogical magazines.

Finding out more

Guild of One-Name Studies (GOONS), www.one-name.org.
An Introduction to Using Computers for Genealogy, David Hawgood, FFHS, 2002
The Female Line, Margaret Ward, Countryside Books, reprinted 2005
Federation of Family History Societies – see Appendix for address and links to county family history societies

Chapter 3

Organising your Research

Keep clear, accurate records of your research right from the start, whether you are using the Internet or visiting record offices and archives. It will save you time, money and frustration in the long term.

Decide what you are looking for

Preparation is the key to efficient, economic research. Each time you use a source, decide whether you are looking for information on just one individual, or whether you want to note every occurrence of that surname you come across. Are you looking at name variants as well? What time period are you restricting yourself to? It will help you to focus your efforts if you give this some thought before you begin.

Use archives and websites efficiently

A letter, phone call or e-mail to the archive you intend to visit will confirm that they do have the records you want to see. In many places it is possible to pre-order documents so that they are ready and waiting for you when you arrive. You may need to book if you have to use a microfilm reader or computer, and sometimes a reader's ticket is necessary before you can see documents, so you will have to have some means of identification with you.

Ask the archive for their research guide, or look at their website for guidance. You will find that there are rules you must follow while you are there. For instance, you will only be able to use a pencil to record notes. Every archive has to take these measures to protect the irreplaceable documents they hold. Many of the most used sources, such as parish registers, are now filmed or fiched to reduce wear and tear on the originals.

If you are using a website for research, take time to look at the background information and tips provided, often in the form of a tour around the site. There may, for instance, be gaps in the coverage and unless you are aware of this, you will not have made a complete search.

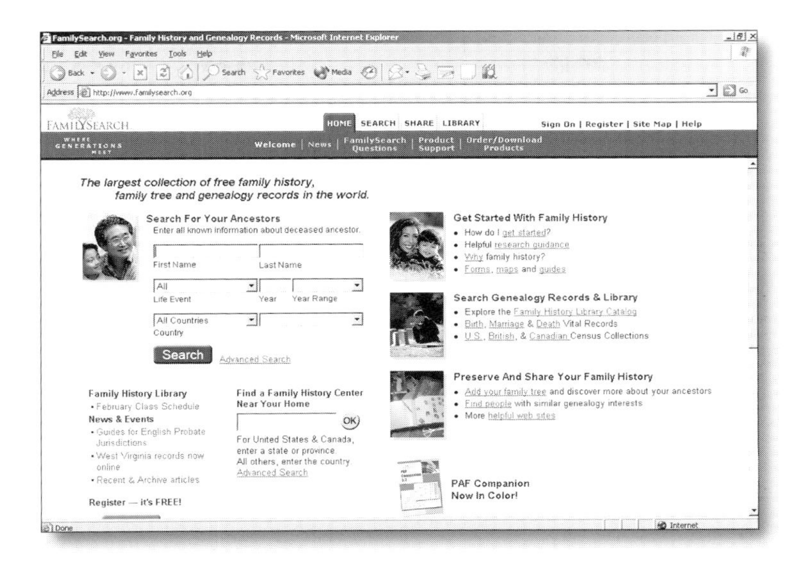

Websites can be useful tools for the family historian but need to be used wisely.

Record, consolidate and preserve your research

Will you remember later what you looked at?

You think you will, but you won't. There is simply too much information to be able to keep everything in your head. When you look back at your notes in a month's time, you must be able to recall exactly what you looked at - and what you did not look at.

Keep a full record of the sources you consult

When you begin each search, note the date, the name of the archive or website, the name(s) you are looking for, the date range of the documents or sources, the document description and reference number, and any other details that will help to pinpoint that day's work in your mind:

23 March 2006 - Hertfordshire Archives and Local Studies - all WARD marriages - DP/64 Kings Langley parish register (microfilm) - marriages 1723 to 1847.

Record surnames in CAPITALS

This is important not only so that you do not make a mistake in the spelling - even when reading your own handwriting - but also to differentiate between names used as middle or family names and the actual surname, e.g. John Lambert SMITH.

Record every word exactly as it appears

Don't abbreviate, or second guess, a name or a phrase, simply write down what you see. 'Jos' may be short for Joseph, or it may be short for Joshua, for instance. If the handwriting is proving difficult, take a photocopy, if that is allowed, or perhaps you will be able to use a digital camera, or print a page out from a website, then look at the entry later, at your leisure.

Finding nothing is important

At the very least it proves that your ancestors were not in a certain place at a certain time! Note negative results as carefully as anything else:

Kings Langley Parish Registers - 1620-1745

Marriages	no WARDs
Baptisms	no WARDs
Burials	no WARDs

Use common abbreviations to save time

But try not to make up your own. Will you remember whether 'b' means born, baptised or buried?

Some common abbreviations

Ag lab	Agricultural labourer
App	Apprentice
B	Born
Bach	Bachelor
Bap	Baptised
Bur	Buried
BTs	Bishops' transcripts
Circa or c.	About (c.1870)

D	Died
Dau	Daughter
Div	Divorced
Dsp	Died without issue, childless (*decessit sine prole*)
Illeg	Illegitimate
Inf	Infant
Inv	Inventory
Lic	Licence
M	Married
MI	Monumental inscription
NK	Not known
Obit	Died
Otp	Of this parish
PR	Parish register
Sp	Spinster
Unm	Unmarried
Wid	Widow or widower

Keeping your records

There are as many filing systems for family history as there are family historians. What's right for one person may be unusable for someone else, so find a way of recording your information that suits you. You will certainly want a file for each individual, possibly within a family group file that keeps siblings together, and to be able to cross-reference records. What about a file for each parish or county, so that you have somewhere to put maps, photographs or local histories that may relate to more than one person or generation? Or keeping all census records together (as well as noted in individual files), or a listing of all references to birth, marriage and death certificates? Having files that bring together a wide range of information relating to, for instance, one surname will sometimes bring surprising new information to light about relationships.

Most people will probably keep their information on a computer and the software will, by necessity, make you enter information in a certain way, but not everything needs to be, or can be, kept on a computer. Where computers score highly is in the ease with which you can create family trees and add new information to files in a tidy way. For up-to-

A simple line pedigree – 'work in progress'

Husband		Wife
John MILBOURNE bap ? bur ?	=	2) Elizabeth CRISP bap ? m 19 Apr 1752 Gt Bealings (Sfk) bur 5 Aug 1773 Gt Bealings (Sfk)
John MILBOURNE bap 5 Nov 1752 Gt Bealings (Sfk) bur ?	=	1) Susannah LUCOCK bap ? m 5 Nov 1777 Grundisburgh (Sfk) bur 8 Sep 1794 Grundisburgh (Sfk)
John MILBOURNE bap 26 Sep 1779 Gt Bealings (Sfk) bur 4 Sep 1868 Woodbridge (Sfk)	=	Martha BUTTON bap ? c1791 m 5 Mar 1804 Woodbridge (Sfk) d Dec qtr 1865 Woodbridge (Sfk)
George MILBOURNE bap 6 Dec 1811 Woodbridge (Sfk) d 18 Sep 1884 Woodbridge (Sfk)	=	Mary Ann CATTERMOLE bap ? m 23 May 1830 Woodbridge (Sfk) bur 22 Sep 1877 Woodbridge (Sfk)
John MILBOURNE b 3 Dec 1837 Woodbridge (Sfk) d 24 May 1875 Woodbridge (Sfk)	=	2) Hannah WIX b ? m 26 Oct 1862 Woodbridge (Sfk) d ?
William Arthur MILBOURNE b 29 Oct 1873 Woodbridge (Sfk) d 4 Aug 1948 Culpho (Sfk)	=	Ellen LAMBERT b 27 Sep 1874 Burgh (Sfk) m 9 Apr 1892 Grundisburgh (Sfk) d 10 Jul 1919 Grundisburgh (Sfk)
Frederick William MILBOURNE b 19 Dec 1892 Grundisburgh (Sfk) d	=	Grace Margaret WALLIS b 13 Mar 1887 Gt Waltham (Ess) m 23 May 1916 Gt Waltham (Ess) d 2 Jul 1959 Chelmsford (Ess)

date information and advice on particular family tree programs, see the various genealogical magazines, or join a FHS and talk to fellow members about what works for them.

A simple line pedigree

It is much easier to make sense of a family tree when it can be drawn out as a diagram. This is where computer software has really come into its own, since it is easy to create a tree at the press of a key and to keep it updated with new information. Drawing a tree by hand is more time-consuming and can be tricky, but many people enjoy the challenge.

A simple line pedigree is shown opposite. The most important rule is to keep it simple and tidy, with clear lines of descent. Keep the more detailed information for your files, where it can be read easily, and just include dates and places of birth/baptism, marriage and death/burial, plus occupations, if you wish. Make sure that these facts have been verified against original sources.

It is quite all right to include partial information or to leave gaps, as long as it is obvious that this is 'work in progress' (see opposite).

The actual line indicating descent descends from the symbol for marriage (=) halfway between a couple. If more than one marriage has taken place, number them (e.g. = 1, or = 2).

Finding out more

Basic Approach to Keeping Your Family Records, Iain Swinnerton, FFHS, 1998

Basic Facts About Archives, Susan B. Lumas, FFHS, 1997

Basic Facts About Using Record Offices for Family Historians, Tom Wood, FFHS, 1999

Family Trees: A Manual for their Design, Layout and Display, Marie Lynskey, Phillimore, 1996

Chapter 4

Names

Before you go any further, have you ever given any thought to what your surname means, or to what it could tell you about your ancestors? And have you realised that your name may have been spelled very differently in the past?

It was not really until the 13th century that surnames, as we are familiar with them, became hereditary for the first time in our history, handed down from father to child. It was only when the population began to grow and people started to move from villages or hamlets, where everyone knew them, to towns or distant parts, where they were strangers, and perhaps most importantly, when the government wanted to make sure that everyone paid their taxes, that it became important to be able to differentiate between the John who lived in the cottage by the wood and John the local blacksmith – and so, John Atwood and John Smith they became.

Surnames

These can be said generally to have originated in four different ways:

1. From a personal name

Calling a man Robertson, for instance, was a way to describe the 'son of Robert', just as Wilson comes from 'son of Will'; Catlin is not so obviously derived from a female ancestor, Katherine.

2. From a place or locality

The ancestors of someone named Kent may have come from that county originally, just as a person named Wallis may have had ancestors in Wales and been known amongst his English neighbours as 'the Welsh'. The name Nash may denote an ancestor who lived by an ash tree ('atten ash'); Milbourne someone who lived by the mill stream.

Usher is an occupational surname (the task today is most often associated with weddings or official functions). Perhaps an undertaker could be said to 'usher' you out of the world? (1853 advertisement)

3. From an occupation

Bakers, Millers, Smiths, Coopers and Butlers can look back to an industrious forebear, though a Hollister may want to overlook the ancestor who was a 'female brothel-keeper'.

4. From a nickname

This might be related to appearance, habits or personality, such as Redhead, Fox, Drinkwater, Black or Brown.

There is a great deal of interesting history to surnames, most of which are by no means so simple to 'read' as the ones given above.

Now that huge quantities of data are becoming available online with census returns, a lot of work is being done on surname distribution. Finding out where there were concentrations of a particular surname in the past may help in pinpointing a place of origin for your family.

Reinventing yourself is not a modern phenomenon and there is nothing to stop anyone living under a different surname to that which they received from their father, as long as they are open about the change and are not doing it with criminal intent. A name change could have come about because of embarrassment (for instance, perfectly good surnames such as Bastard or Piddle might not have been welcomed by an upwardly-mobile Victorian family), or fear, as happened when many German names were hurriedly anglicised at the start of the First World War.

Just because you share a surname with a famous person from the past, it is no guarantee that you come from the same family. Always work backward from what you know and never try to force a link that does not exist in the original records.

Women, of course, continue to change their surnames with irritating frequency. In the distant past, daughterhood, marriage, motherhood, widowhood or inheritance could have an effect on a woman's name. Today, marriage, divorce, widowhood, remarriage, or professional status can all bring about changes. Women's surnames sometimes live on in a family as middle names – an unusual second or third name can be a useful clue to a family connection.

'We've always spelled it this way'

You will soon realise that it is dangerous to assume that your surname has 'always' been spelled in a particular way. Consider the journey it has made through the centuries. In that time it has been bandied about in a thick local accent, misheard and misspelled by umpteen disinterested clerks or parsons, and wrongly transcribed by more bored underlings in government offices – and, until the late 19th century, it is doubtful that your ancestors would have known, or cared, if the name was being spelled 'wrongly' anyway, since the majority could not read or write.

People in the past were quite relaxed about spelling, and it is not uncommon to read a document in which a name is spelled in two or more different ways on the same page (written by the same person). These are known as name variants. Some indexes take account of possible variations, some do not and it is up to you to check. Never be too restrictive in your searches and never make the mistake of saying, 'We've always spelled it this way.'

First names

First names can be as interesting as surnames. Some families seem to have a naming pattern, which they follow through the generations, perhaps naming the first boy after the father, the second after the paternal grandfather, the third after the maternal grandfather, and so on, with an equivalent for the girls. If you notice such a pattern in your family, it can be an aid to identification.

Fashion and popular events can also have their effects on naming babies, just as they do today. Sometimes, a name can give you a surprising

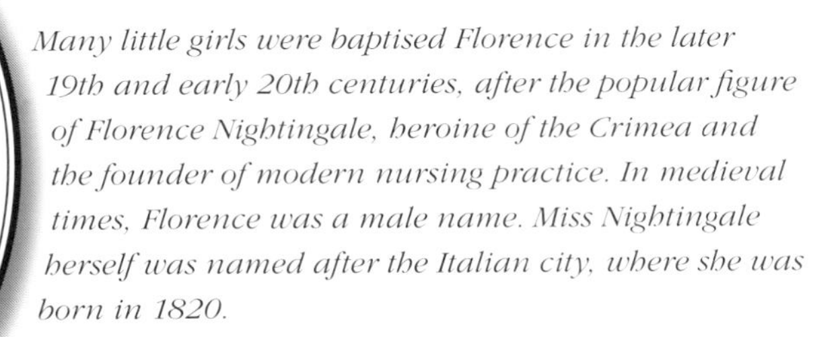

Many little girls were baptised Florence in the later 19th and early 20th centuries, after the popular figure of Florence Nightingale, heroine of the Crimea and the founder of modern nursing practice. In medieval times, Florence was a male name. Miss Nightingale herself was named after the Italian city, where she was born in 1820.

insight into an ancestor's political feelings – as boys from the 1800s named Napoleon after the French general and emperor (and enemy of Britain) demonstrate.

It was not uncommon in the past for successive babies to be given the same name, one after the other. In most cases this probably means that the first baby of that name died, so another little Henry, or John, was welcomed into the family. But you should not assume this to be the case without evidence. Some parents just seemed to like certain names. It doesn't mean that the children were actually called by that baptismal name as they grew up – one family historian found that the grandfather she knew as Samuel, who had answered to that name all his life, was baptised John, as were his older brother and his father. No doubt they were known by entirely different names, too!

Finding out more

Searching for Surnames, John Titford, Countryside Books, 2002
Oxford Dictionary of English Surnames, P.H. Reaney and R.M. Wilson, OUP, 1997
Surnames and Genealogy: A New Approach, George Redmonds, FFHS, 2002
Family Names and Family History, David Hey, Hambledon & London, 2000
Christian Names in Local and Family History, George Redmonds, TNA, 2004
First Name Variants, Alan Bardsley, FFHS, 2nd ed, 2003

Chapter 5

Births, Marriages and Deaths

Civil registration

The official records of births, marriages and deaths in England and Wales since 1837 are the essential links that will allow you to draw up the early stages of your family tree. In that year the country was divided into about 500 registration districts (RDs), each under the supervision of a superintendent registrar, with a further breakdown into sub-districts under registrars. That system of recording births, marriages and deaths still continues today (see Chapter 14 for Scotland and Ireland).

Births and deaths are reported to the local registrar by an individual with a connection to the event, and marriages are recorded by the clergyman performing the ceremony or the local registrar who performs a civil wedding (there have been some changes over the years, see Marriages below).

Local register offices still hold copies of certificates and have their own indexing system. If you know your ancestors were born, married and died in a particular locality, it may be worthwhile searching in the local register office rather than the national indexes. There are fees for this, and you must appreciate that the Registrar's first priority is to those who are registering current events. To find the whereabouts of current register offices, there is a link on www.gro.gov.uk, which also has details of fees and searches. There are ongoing projects to transcribe original certificates held at local register offices; a list of links with county websites can be found at www.ukbmd.org.uk.

The national index was created from the copy certificates forwarded every three months by the superintendent registrars to the Registrar General at the General Register Office. Quarterly indexes were then created at the GRO (until 1984 when they were computerised and published annually), separately for births, marriages and deaths. These are known as the March quarter (January to March registrations); the June quarter (April to June); the September quarter (July to September); and the December quarter (October to December).

Within these volumes, names appear in alphabetical order, giving surname, forename, registration district, volume number and page number. It is sometimes not easy to decide whether a particular registration district falls within the area you are interested in, but the counties were all given a code number in 1837 (listed overleaf) which allows you, for instance, to see at a glance that 'Plomesgate 4a' is in Essex or Suffolk.

What is known as the GRO reference number, which you will need to be able to order a certificate, consists of the Quarter, Year, District, Volume and Page Number. (If you do approach the local register office, the GRO reference number is of no use as it uses a different system of filing - and to find a marriage you will need to know the church where the ceremony took place.)

New family historians often only encounter the GRO index books online, as a searchable, digitalised database, rather than by struggling with the heavy volumes, now held at the Family Records Centre, that built up the muscles of so many genealogists in times past. If you can, you should visit the FRC at least once, if only to experience the real thing!

Searching the GRO indexes and ordering certificates

The indexes can be searched in various ways:

1. On open shelves at the Family Records Centre, where they can be seen free of charge.
2. On microfiche: sets will be found at County Record Offices and major libraries around the country, again free of charge to consult.
3. On several websites offering searchable, digitalised images of the index pages:

   www.freebmd.org.uk - volunteers are gradually putting transcriptions of the pages (rather than digitalised images) onto this website, which is free to use. Coverage is now almost complete to 1911, but you should check the information on the website before you begin.
   www.ancestry.co.uk www.findmypast.com
   www.familyrelatives.org

GRO REGISTRATION DISTRICTS

For the GRO indexes the country was divided into areas, each with its own volume code number. Knowing the volume number can be a great help when deciding whether an index entry is the right one, as the locations of registration districts are not always immediately recognisable.

1837-1851

I	London & Middlesex
II	London & Middlesex
III	London & Middlesex
IV	London & Surrey
V	Kent
VI	Bedfordshire, Berkshire, Buckinghamshire & Hertfordshire
VII	Hampshire & Sussex
VIII	Dorset, Hampshire & Wiltshire
IX	Cornwall & Devon
X	Devon & Somerset
XI	Gloucestershire, Somerset & Warwickshire
XII	Essex & Suffolk
XIII	Norfolk & Suffolk
XIV	Cambridgeshire, Huntingdonshire & Lincolnshire
XV	Leicestershire, Northamptonshire, Nottinghamshire & Rutland
XVI	Oxfordshire, Staffordshire & Warwickshire
XVII	Staffordshire
XVIII	Gloucestershire, Shropshire, Staffordshire, Warwickshire & Worcestershire
XIX	Cheshire, Derbyshire & Flintshire
XX	Lancashire
XXI	Lancashire & Yorkshire
XXII	Yorkshire
XXIII	Yorkshire
XXIV	Durham & Yorkshire
XXV	Cumberland, Lancashire, Northumberland & Westmorland
XXVI	Brecknockshire, Carmarthenshire, Glamorganshire, Herefordshire,

www.bmdindex.co.uk
www.TheGenealogist.co.uk

Once you have found the entry in the index, you can order a certificate:-

in person at the Family Records Centre in London;

by post from the GRO, PO Box 2, Southport, Merseyside PR8 2JD (cheques must be made payable to 'ONS');

by phone on 0845 603 7788;

or online at www.gro.gov.uk.

Monmouthshire, Pembrokeshire, Radnorshire & Shropshire
XXVII Anglesey, Caernarvonshire, Cardinganshire, Denbighshire, Flintshire, Merionethshire & Montgomeryshire

(These Roman numerals were gradually replaced by Arabic numbering as the early, handwritten, index volumes were retyped and rebound.)

1852-August 1946

1a-c	London & Middlesex
1d	London, Kent & Surrey
2a	Kent & Surrey
2b	Hampshire & Sussex
2c	Berkshire & Hampshire
3a	Berkshire, Buckinghamshire, Hertfordshire, Middlesex & Oxfordshire
3b	Bedfordshire, Cambridgeshire, Huntingdonshire, Northamptonshire & Suffolk
4a	Essex & Suffolk
4b	Norfolk
5a	Dorset & Wiltshire
5b	Devon
5c	Cornwall & Somerset
6a	Gloucestershire, Herefordshire & Shropshire
6b	Staffordshire, Warwickshire & Worcestershire
6c	Warwickshire & Worcestershire
6d	Warwickshire
7a	Leicestershire, Lincolnshire & Rutland
7b	Derbyshire & Nottinghamshire
8a	Cheshire
8b-d	Lancashire
9a-d	Yorkshire
10a	Durham
10b	Cumberland, Northumberland & Westmorland
11a	Glamorganshire, Monmouthshire & Pembrokeshire
11b	Anglesey, Brecknockshire, Denbighshire, Flintshire, Montgomeryshire & Radnorshire

Unless you want the GRO staff to search the indexes for you, which is more expensive, you will need to be able to quote the full name and the GRO reference number. The cheapest option is to order online or in person at the FRC (currently £7); by post or phone it will cost £8.50. The certificate will be posted to you within a few days. Details of prices and the options available to you are on the official website above.

The indexes and certificates since 1837

Births

A birth certificate will, hopefully, give you the information you need to find the parents' marriage certificate and go one generation further back in your family tree.

BIRTHS AND DEATHS REGISTRATION ACT, 1874.

CERTIFICATE OF REGISTRY OF BIRTH.

I, the undersigned, Do hereby certify that the Birth of Diana Margaret Milbourne born on the 20 day of January One thousand nine hundred and (a) twenty has been duly registered by me at Entry No. 441 of my Register Book No. 1 (a) Insert year in words.

Witness my hand, this 26 day of January 1920

Fred Turner } Registrar of Births and Deaths.

District Chelmsford Sub-District Chelmsford Borough

NOTICE.

This Certificate when duly filled up by the Registrar, is to be given (on demand) to the INFORMANT at the time of Registering the Birth, on payment of a fee not exceeding Three-pence. (See Births and Deaths Registration Act, 1874, Section 30.)

—Printed by Authority of the Registrar General by McCorquodale & Co., Ltd.—

A short birth certificate will give very little useful information; always apply for the full certificate. (Reproduced with the permission of the Controller of HMSO)

The **GRO index** states:

- the baby's full name (with initials instead of middle names from the September quarter 1911 to the December quarter 1965);
- the mother's maiden name (from the September quarter 1911);
- the registration district where the birth took place;
- and the GRO reference number.

The ***birth certificate*** has the following information:

When and where born – The date of birth and an address. This may be the family home, or it may be a workhouse or hospital (or, in the 20th century, a nursing home), so this will not necessarily tell you the home address. If a time of birth is noted, it may indicate a multiple birth.

Name, if any - Parents did not have to make a decision on the baby's name when they registered the birth, so it was possible to add or change a name up to one year after registration. Once baptised, however, the name could not be altered. Babies not named can be found at the end of each alphabetical list as 'male' or 'female', so always check there if you cannot find an entry.

Name and surname of father - If no name appears here, it will indicate an illegitimate birth. The mother could simply give a name for the claimed father before 1875, but after that date he had to agree to be identified as the father of her illegitimate child and come with her to the register office or sign an affidavit. After 1969, the father's place of birth is included.

Name, surname and maiden surname of mother - This will tell you if the baby's mother was married before, giving her present surname, any previous married name, and her maiden name. After 1969, her place of birth is also noted.

Occupation of father - It can be helpful to know the father's occupation as a way of differentiating between two or more men with similar names. After 1984 the mother's occupation is also recorded although of course most women worked through much of their married life, it simply was not acknowledged.

Signature, description and residence of informant - Usually this is the mother or father, but a different name could alert you to other connections, such as a married sister.

When registered - From 1875 registration of births was made compulsory (indicating that many births were missed in the years before) and registration had to take place within six weeks of the birth. After those 42 days, a fee was payable. There is no doubt that some parents simply ignored the law, perhaps believing that baptism was sufficient.

Name entered after registration - See above.

CB 945853

CERTIFIED COPY of an EN[TRY OF BIRTH]
Pursuant to the Births and Deaths Re[gistration Act]

The Statutory Fee for this Certificate is 2s. 6d. together with 1d. Stamp Duty. Where a search is necessary to find the entry, a Search Fee is payable in addition.

Registration District Woodbridge

1893. Birth in the Sub-District of Carlford **in the** ...

Columns:—	1	2	3	4	5	6
No.	When and Where Born.	Name, if any.	Sex.	Name and Surname of Father.	Name and Maiden Surname of Mother.	Rank or Profession of Father.
197	Nineteenth December 1892 Grundisburgh R.S.D.	Frederick William	Boy	William Arthur Milbourne	Ellen Milbourne formerly Lambert	Groom & Jobmaster

I, R.S. Kell, Superintendent Registrar for the District of Deben do hereby certify that this is a true copy of the Entry No. 197 in the Register Book of Births No. 24 for the ... in my custody.

WITNESS MY HAND this 22nd day of March, 1947.

CAUTION.—Any person who (1) falsifies any of the particulars on this Certificate, or (2) uses it as true, knowing it to be falsified, is liable to Prosecution.

Marriages

Begin your search in the quarter a known child is born and work backwards through the years. It may be a long search as a woman's child-bearing years could be twenty or more. If you don't find the marriage by these means, go forwards in time – perhaps the couple did not marry until after one or several of their children were born. They may, of course, never have married at all. If you know the surnames of both parties then search for the more unusual name – it will be quicker to find in the indexes. Once you have the information on a marriage certificate, you can look for the birth certificates of bride and groom, and go back another generation.

In 1837 when civil registration began, marriages were only recognised if they were performed by a Church of England clergyman in the parish church; in a Quaker meeting house; in a Jewish synagogue; or in the local register office by the registrar. If the event was performed in a chapel by

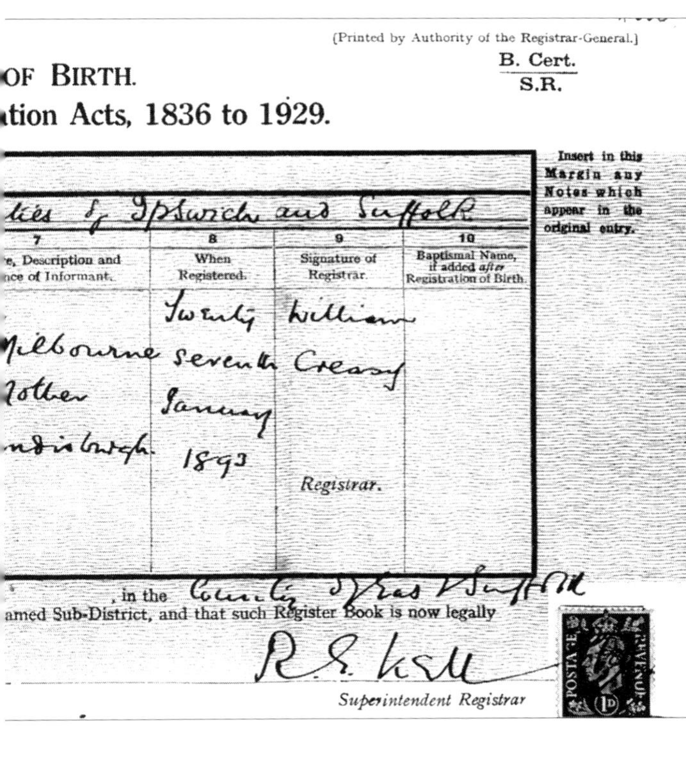
[Printed by Authority of the Registrar-General.]

B. Cert.
S.R.

OF BIRTH.
ation Acts, 1836 to 1929.

Insert in this Margin any Notes which appear in the original entry.

ties of Ipswich and Suffolk

7	8	9	10
e, Description and nce of Informant.	When Registered.	Signature of Registrar.	Baptismal Name, if added after Registration of Birth.
Milbourne Mother ndis borough	Twenty seventh January 1893	William Creasy Registrar.	

, in the County of Eas Suffolk
amed Sub-District, and that such Register Book is now legally

Superintendent Registrar

The birth certificate for Frederick William Milbourne records his father's full name and his mother's maiden name, which gives the information needed to search for their marriage certificate. (Reproduced with the permission of the Controller of HMSO)

a nonconformist minister or in a Roman Catholic church by a Catholic priest, the registrar also had to attend, but this condition ended in 1898 when nonconformist ministers and Catholic priests were given the same status as Anglican ministers in the eyes of the law.

The **GRO index** gives you:

- the names of the bride and bridegroom, individually listed alphabetically (from March 1912 each entry also shows the surname of the other party);
- the registration district where the marriage took place;
- and the GRO reference number.

The ***marriage certificate*** tells you, for both individuals:

The place of marriage, e.g. 'the Parish Church in the Parish of Great Waltham in the County of Essex'.

When married – the date and year.

Name and surname – for a widow, hers may be the surname of her last husband (and therefore different to her father's surname which will, of course, give her maiden name).

Age – this could just be 'of full age' or 'minor' (i.e. over or under 21) but this may have been deliberately vague and is not necessarily true. People often fibbed about their ages when they got married so don't be too rigid about what you expect. Up to 1929, boys could marry at the age

P/2 706584

The Statutory Fee for this Certificate is 2s. 7d. If required subsequently to registration, a Search Fee is payable in addition.

CERTIFIED COPY of an ENTRY OF

Pursuant to the Marriage Acts, 18

Registration District Chelmsford.

1940. Marriage Solemnized at S. Peter's Church of the Ascension Chelmsford in the County of

Columns :— No.	1 When Married.	2 Name and Surname.	3 Age.	4 Condition.	5 Rank or Profession.	Residence
68	19th June 1940.	Frederick George Orchin	23	Bachelor	Soldier	109. Ch
		Diana Margaret Milbourne	20	Spinster	—	76, C

Married in the above church according to the Rites and Ceremonies of the Church of

This Marriage was solemnized between us, Frederick George Orchin, Diana Margaret Milbourne

in the Presence of us, Arthur M. Edwards, Margaret G. Milbourne, Susan Orchin

I, David Ford, Curate of the Ascension, Chelmsford in th

a true copy of the Entry No. 68, in the Register Book of Marriages of the said Church.

WITNESS MY HAND this 19th day of June 1940..

CAUTION.—Any person who (1) falsifies any of the particulars on this Certificate, or (2) uses it as true, knowing it to be falsified, is liable to Prosecution.

of 14, and girls at 12 (though rarely did so), but then the minimum age was increased to 16 for both sexes.

Condition – whether bachelor/spinster, or widower/widow. Late 19th-century and 20th-century certificates may state 'divorced', and should give the name of the ex-spouse.

Rank or Profession – occupation. A woman's occupation was rarely recorded in the past. But this did not mean that she did not work.

Residence at the time of marriage – this could be in the bride's home parish if she went home to marry, and not necessarily where the couple normally lived. Sometimes the address is vague, perhaps just 'Great

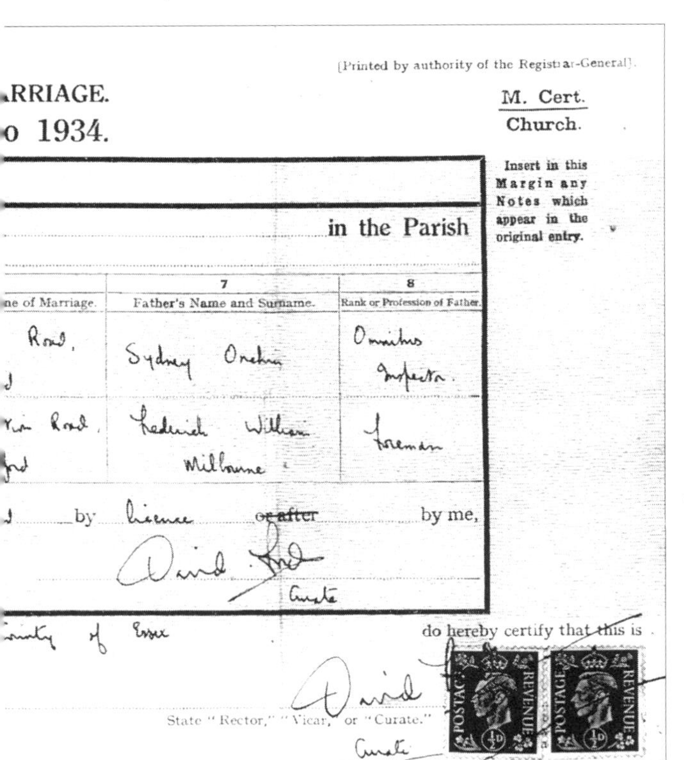
[Printed by authority of the Registrar-General].

RRIAGE.
o 1934.

M. Cert.
Church.

Insert in this Margin any Notes which appear in the original entry.

in the Parish

ne of Marriage.	7 Father's Name and Surname.	8 Rank or Profession of Father.
Road,	Sydney Orchin	Omnibus Inspector
Road,	Frederick William Milbourne	Foreman

by Licence ~~or after~~ by me,

David [illegible]
Curate

County of Essex

do hereby certify that ~~this~~ is

David [illegible]

State "Rector," "Vicar," or "Curate."
Curate

The original marriage certificate of Frederick Orchin and Diana Milbourne in June 1940. The marriage was by licence, as the bridegroom had been rescued from the beaches at Dunkirk only days earlier. The creases in the certificate show how keeping such documents folded away in envelopes may mark them and eventually shorten their life. (Reproduced with the permission of the Controller of HMSO)

Waltham'. The couple would have to live in a parish for four weeks if they wanted to marry by banns, but the banns may have been called in both parishes of residence.

Father's name and surname – never the mother's name. It may say 'deceased', which is useful, but lack of that word is not proof that the father is still alive. If no name is given, it may mean illegitimacy, but it may also be because the bride or groom never knew their father, who died before they were born.

Rank or Profession of Father – occupation.

Whether the marriage was 'by Licence' or 'after Banns' – banns were proclaimed publicly in church every Sunday for three weeks before a marriage was performed, so that any objections could be made. Getting a licence was a more private and quicker way to marry, but probably too expensive for most people.

The signatures of the bride and groom – they may make their mark with an 'X' if unable to write (but an 'X' does not necessarily mean that the person was illiterate – a woman, for instance, may have hesitated to sign if her new husband could not).

The signatures of at least two witnesses – who may be relatives, perhaps brothers or sisters, or friends. There were, however, 'professional witnesses' who could be called in if a couple did not have anyone nearby to stand up with them – or even a passer-by might be drafted in at a pinch!

Deaths

Sometimes family historians ignore death certificates, perhaps because they feel that they do not add anything to help create the family tree. However, not only will you find out what your ancestor died of, but you could also discover an address that will help you when searching the census, or the name of a relative. It may even lead to a newspaper obituary or a report on a coroner's inquest.

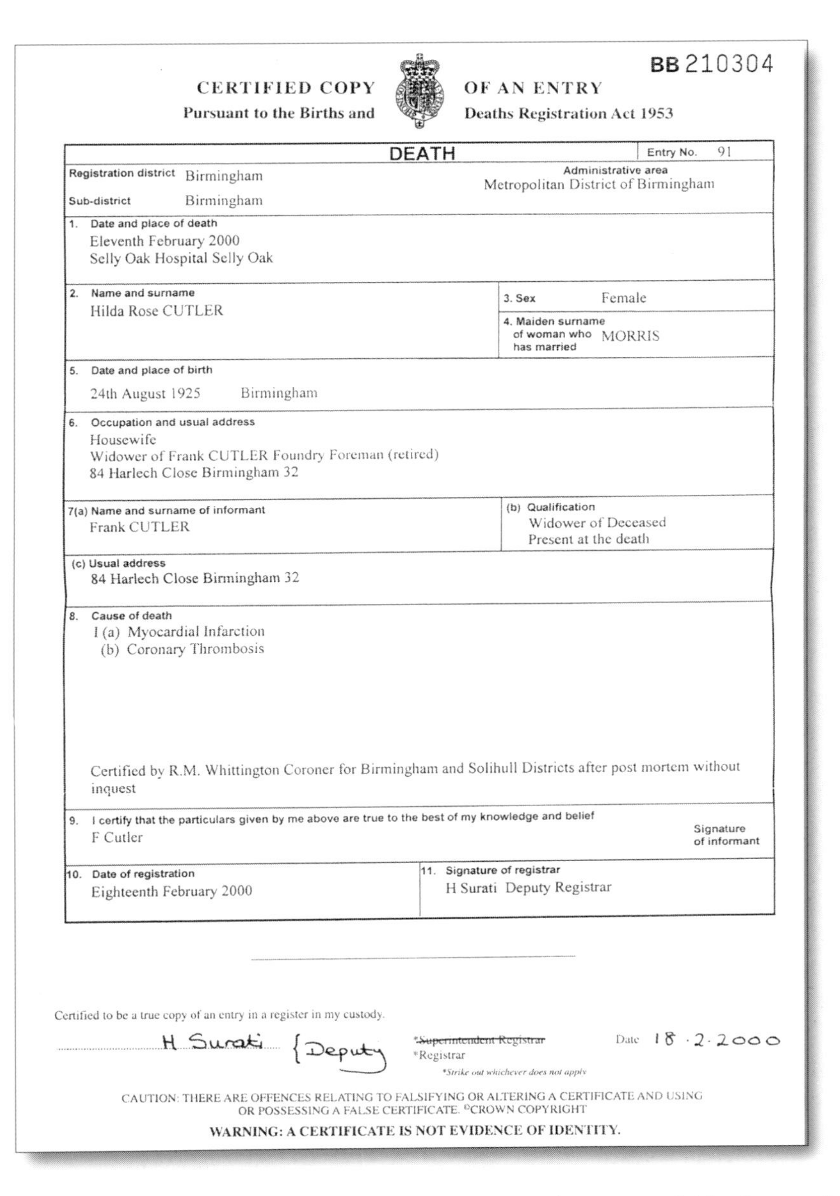

BB 210304

CERTIFIED COPY OF AN ENTRY
Pursuant to the Births and Deaths Registration Act 1953

DEATH — Entry No. 91

Registration district: Birmingham
Administrative area: Metropolitan District of Birmingham
Sub-district: Birmingham

1. Date and place of death
Eleventh February 2000
Selly Oak Hospital Selly Oak

2. Name and surname
Hilda Rose CUTLER

3. Sex: Female

4. Maiden surname of woman who has married: MORRIS

5. Date and place of birth
24th August 1925 Birmingham

6. Occupation and usual address
Housewife
Widower of Frank CUTLER Foundry Foreman (retired)
84 Harlech Close Birmingham 32

7(a) Name and surname of informant
Frank CUTLER

(b) Qualification
Widower of Deceased
Present at the death

(c) Usual address
84 Harlech Close Birmingham 32

8. Cause of death
I (a) Myocardial Infarction
(b) Coronary Thrombosis

Certified by R.M. Whittington Coroner for Birmingham and Solihull Districts after post mortem without inquest

9. I certify that the particulars given by me above are true to the best of my knowledge and belief
F Cutler — Signature of informant

10. Date of registration
Eighteenth February 2000

11. Signature of registrar
H Surati Deputy Registrar

Certified to be a true copy of an entry in a register in my custody.

H Surati {Deputy ~~*Superintendent Registrar~~ *Registrar — Date 18·2·2000

*Strike out whichever does not apply

CAUTION: THERE ARE OFFENCES RELATING TO FALSIFYING OR ALTERING A CERTIFICATE AND USING OR POSSESSING A FALSE CERTIFICATE. ©CROWN COPYRIGHT

WARNING: A CERTIFICATE IS NOT EVIDENCE OF IDENTITY.

A death certificate, even a very recent one, can provide some useful background information. (Reproduced with the permission of the Controller of HMSO)

You may have a long search for the certificate if you do not know when your ancestor died. (The census can help here. If a person is found, perhaps, in the 1861 census but not in the 1871 one, then your search could be directed to those ten years.) People did live longer than we tend to believe – if they survived the dangerous years of infancy and childhood they were just as likely to live to a ripe old age as we are nowadays. Registration of a death may have been delayed, and so appear in a later quarter than you expect, if there has been a post mortem or inquest, which should be noted on the certificate itself. Unidentified bodies are listed as 'Unknown' at the end of the quarter – not much help to a family historian!

The **GRO index** gives you:

- the name of the deceased;
- the age at death (from the March quarter 1866 to the March quarter 1969, then the date of birth);
- the registration district where he or she died;
- and the GRO reference number.

The ***death certificate*** tells you:
When and where died – not necessarily where the person normally lived, nor where they were finally buried.

Full name – from 1969 also the maiden name of a married woman.

Age at death – given from the March quarter 1866 to the March quarter 1969, and from then on the date of birth instead (and the place of birth). Treat ages with caution – the person registering the death may simply have been the occupier of the house where the event took place and not have known much about the deceased. For children it should be accurate as it had to be either the father or mother who registered the death.

Occupation – this may be the father's occupation in the case of a child's death; on the certificate of a woman there may simply be a note 'wife of ...' or 'widow of...'.

Cause of death - from 1874 death had to be certified by a doctor before the certificate could be issued. If there had to be an inquest, this will be noted here.

Signature, description and residence of informant - can be a relative, or a doctor, or other official such as a workhouse master or, simply, a neighbour. It will often say 'present at the death' but this may just mean the person was on the premises at the time.

When registered - the registration may have been delayed by the need for a post mortem or inquest.

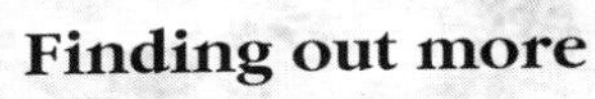

Finding out more

An Introduction to British Civil Registration, Tom Wood, FFHS, 2nd ed, 2000
Basic Facts about Using the Family Records Centre, Audrey Collins, FFHS, 1998
The Family Records Centre: A User's Guide, Stella Colwell, TNA, 2002
Basic Facts About Using Baptism Records for Family Historians, Pauline Litton, FFHS, 1996
Basic Facts About Using Marriage Records for Family Historians, Pauline Litton, FFHS, 1996
Basic Facts About Using Death and Burial Records for Family Historians, Lilian Gibbens, FFHS, 2nd ed, 1999

Maps showing the location of registration districts are available from the Institute of Heraldic & Genealogical Studies, 79-82 Northgate, Canterbury, Kent CT1 1BA (telephone 01227 765617; website www.ihgs.ac.uk); alternatively, there are historical lists of districts and sub-districts at www.fhsc.org.uk/genuki/reg

Chapter 6

The Census

The census is unique. Other records may relate to an individual, or perhaps to a couple, but here is your family, hopefully all together at home, on one night in the year over a century ago. What you discover can supplement your searches for births, marriages and deaths, and may help you track down a particularly awkward ancestor or reveal an extended family. With national name indexes increasingly available, finding your ancestors on census night has never been easier.

The British government has taken a census of the population every ten years since 1801 (1821 in Ireland; see Chapter 14 for comments on the Irish and Scottish census returns). That first census revealed a population of 10 million people in England and Wales and by 1901 over 32 million names were included, while 200 years later, in 2001, that figure had multiplied to 60 million.

To ensure privacy, the information from each census is closed for 100 years after which, on the first working day following the centenary, it is opened to public access. The 1901 census is now available and the next release will be that of the 1911 census in January 2012. Only in 1941 was no national census taken, because of the Second World War.

The census returns from 1801 to 1831 are of little genealogical value, unfortunately, as the object was only to provide a numerical return of households. However, the count was based on the parish and was put into the hands of the local clergyman or overseer of the poor, and some of these individuals produced returns that went far beyond their official brief, listing residents individually. You may be lucky enough to find one of these local returns for your area preserved at the county record office.

The census since 1841

Since 1841, taking the census in England and Wales has been the responsibility of Superintendent Registrars employed by the General Register Office (GRO), which created the new enumeration districts.

In that year, paid census enumerators were employed for the first time. These men (women were not employed as enumerators until 1891) had the difficult task of visiting each of the 250 or so houses in their enumeration district, first to deliver the new census forms (schedules), designed to be 'self-completed', and then to collect them, hopefully correctly filled in.

In practice, the enumerator himself had to complete many forms for illiterate householders, and to deal with those who just wouldn't cooperate. Even with all the modern finding aids, there is always the chance that you will be unable to find your ancestor in the census returns. Consider the impenetrable accents and local dialects he faced, for one thing. If he simply wrote down what he heard, or guessed at what he had heard, there was ample scope for a name or a birthplace to be recorded wrongly. The householder may not have been too sure about his facts, either.

The enumerator copied the information on the householders' forms into his census enumerator's book (CEB), which is the source of the images we see today (and whenever a copy of a document is made, error can creep in). The CEBs appear in the records arranged by registration districts (the same ones already encountered with birth, marriage and death certificates), and then by sub-districts. Each book has a page at the front where the enumerator describes the route he travelled to collect the schedules, and this can be useful if, for instance, you want to know roughly where in a village without street names your ancestors' cottage was located. To see this page you will have to look at the filmed copies rather than the online images.

What the census tells you

The questions asked of householders on census night included:

- surname, first name and, from 1851 onwards, middle names (although usually recorded only as initials).
- age at last birthday (in 1841 ages were recorded differently; accurate up to 15, then rounded down to the nearest five, so that, for instance, age 23 appears as 20, age 48 as 45). Ages can be notoriously inaccurate, however, so take them with a pinch of salt.

Ancestors who 'lived in' at their workplace will have been recorded there on census night.

- marital status, i.e. married, unmarried, widow(er).
- relationship to the head of household, e.g. wife, son-in-law, servant, lodger (1851 onwards).
- rank, profession or occupation. In other words, their source of income, so this includes pensioners, 'living on own means', etc. From 1851 farmers also provided details of the acreage farmed and, together with other employers, the number of men and boys employed, while from 1891 the question of whether employed, self-employed or employer was asked. In 1901, it was additionally noted whether working from home. Children were recorded as scholar or student (from 1851 to 1871).

- birthplace. In 1841 this was simply a 'Yes' or 'No' to the question of whether born in that same county, with 'S' to denote born in Scotland, 'I' for Ireland, and 'F' for 'foreign parts'. From 1851, it should give the parish and county, or country of birth. This is another detail to be treated with caution. Many people probably could not remember their actual place of birth, and many more doctored the information, particularly the elderly who may have feared being sent back to their place of settlement under the Poor Laws.

The information also included:

- the number of rooms in the household, if fewer than five (from 1891), a reaction to the government's concern about overcrowding in the cities.
- infirmities, i.e. whether deaf, dumb or blind (from 1851), and whether mentally afflicted (from 1871).
- in Wales only, whether Welsh-speaking.

A census return for 1851, from St Margaret's, Ipswich. (The National Archives: ref: H0107/1800 f.583)

Parish ~~or Township~~ of St Margaret | ~~Ecclesiastical District of~~ | ~~City or~~ Borough of Ipswich | ~~Town of~~ | ~~Village of~~

No. of Householder's Schedule	Name of Street, Place, or Road, and Name or No. of House	Name and Surname of each Person who abode in the house, on the Night of the 30th March, 1851	Relation to Head of Family	Condition	Age of Males	Age of Females	Rank, Profession, or Occupation	Where Born	Whether Blind, or Deaf-and-Dumb
5	Permit Office Court	Henry Frost	Head	Mar	30		Bricklayer (Journeyman)	Suffolk Ipswich	
		Maria R Do	Wife	Mar		29		Do Do	
		Lucy Milbourne	Visitor	U		28	Gloveress	Do Do	
6	Permit Office Court	David Debney	Head	Mar	47		(Carpenter (Journeyman)	Suffolk Ipswich	
		Sarah Do	Wife	Mar		47		Do Do	
		David Do	Son	U	20		Carpenter (Journeyman)	Do Do	
		Charles Do	Son	U	17		Do Do	Do Do	
		George Do	Son		13		Scholar	Do Do	
		Ellen Do	Daur			6	Do	Do Do	
7	Permit Office Court	Harriet Easter	Head	Widow		61	Charwoman	Suffolk Ipswich	
		Elizabeth Do	Daur	U		27	Housemaid	Do Do	
		Eliza Do	Daur	U		18	Staymaker	Do Do	
		John Barker	Visitor		3		Scholar		
8	Permit Office Court	Joseph Bugg	Head	Mar	31		Foundry Warehouseman	Suffolk Ipswich	
		Ann Do	Wife	Mar		31		Do Do	
		Caroline Do	Daur			9	Scholar	Do Do	

Total of Houses: 4 U B | Total of Persons: 7 9

B—Eng.

Tracing your family in the census may boost your research in many ways. Finding someone's age on a census return, for instance, can help you trace their birth certificate or baptism; in earlier censuses the information may take you back well into the 18th century (someone aged 80 in 1851, for example, will have been born in about 1771).

The census also helps to narrow down other search areas. If, for instance, someone is unmarried in 1861 and married in 1871, you can search those ten years in the GRO indexes for a marriage certificate. If the children of a marriage have different birthplaces, it gives you an idea how long they have been living there and where else they had travelled round the country. Relatives staying overnight could alert you to other parts of the family, or to the wife's family and maiden name. A grandchild staying may lead you to a daughter's married name.

Follow good practice when consulting the census and note down the exact reference for the information you find (or note if you have looked and been unsuccessful). Each census page has a National Archives reference number:

1841 (6 June) HO 107;
1851 (30 March) HO 107;
1861 (7 April) RG 9;
1871 (2 April) RG 10;
1881 (3 April) RG 11;
1891 (5 April) RG 12;
1901 (31 March) RG 13.

There is also a piece number (relating to the enumerator's folder), a folio number (stamped on the top right-hand corner of each page) and a page number. With these you can track down any census page again. Note also the enumeration district and other locality details, given at the top of the page, and the householder's schedule number (not to be confused with a street number, in the left-hand column). All these references are usually given in full on the various indexes.

Where to find the census

There is an almost bewildering choice of census material available today, and new indexes and transcripts are being brought out all the time. The best way to keep up-to-date with what is new is to read one of the family history magazines, visit TNA's website, or search on the Internet via a good search engine.

The following serves merely as an introduction to the main sources:

- The national census returns from 1841 to 1901 are held on microfilm/ microfiche at the Family Records Centre, where there is also a good collection of name and street indexes. The 1901 census is also at The National Archives at Kew. County Record Offices will hold film of all censuses for their areas, and large county libraries often have filmed copies of the census for their vicinity, too. These are free to view.
- A large number of county returns from all census years, with page images, are available to buy on CD-ROM, some with indexes, from companies such as Archive CD Books, Stepping Stones, and S&N Genealogy (see Appendix).
- The major websites with name indexes linked to digitalized page images are:

  The National Archives - www.1901censusonline.com (1901), and www.nationalarchives.gov.uk/census for 1891, 1881, 1871, 1861, 1851 and 1841, in association with Ancestry.com.

  www.ancestry.co.uk for 1901, 1891, 1881, 1871, 1861, 1851 and 1841.

  www.findmypast.com for 1841,1861,1871 and 1891.

  www.TheGenealogist.co.uk for census indexes and transcripts 1841 to 1901.
- The LDS Church Family History Centres (see Appendix) can order census films for you to view. The 1881 census index and transcript is available from them on CD-ROM (write to LDS Distribution Centre, 399 Garretts Green Lane, Birmingham B33 0UH; telephone 08700 102051 - current price £29.95). The 1881 census is also searchable on the LDS website, www.familysearch.org, completely free of charge.

- Family History Societies often have indexes and transcripts, in booklet, fiche or CD format, particularly of the 1851 census. Many census records (and all the 1881) are on www.familyhistoryonline.net, but varying in details and coverage from one county to another (pay-per-view).
- FreeCEN is a group of volunteers working to put census returns on the net, freely available. There is only a very limited coverage as yet, but you may be lucky – www.freecen.org.uk.

Indexes to the censuses have made them much more accessible in the last few years and a few minutes on the Internet can now solve problems that would once have taken twenty years of painstaking research. As with all indexes, however, they are only as good as the records themselves and the people who transcribed them. Would you have expected to find Joseph transcribed as 'Zaresh', or Emily indexed as 'Smiley'? Each index gives tips on how to make the most of your search and on the use of, for instance, wildcards. It is well worth spending a few minutes familiarising yourself with the instructions.

And, of course, your ancestor may have been living under another name, or sleeping rough, or travelling overnight and so been missed by the enumerator. He may have been out of the country, or in prison and only recorded by his initials. It is estimated that up to 10% of the population was missed off the 1861 census and it is a certainty that many slipped through the net every ten years, just as they do today.

Finding out more

Local Census Listings 1522-1930 Jeremy Gibson & Mervyn Medlycott, FFHS, 3rd ed reprinted 2001

Making Use of the Census, Susan Lumas, PRO, 4th ed, 2002

Making Sense of the Census Revisited: Census Records for England and Wales 1801-1901, Edward Higgs, TNA, 2005

The Family Records Centre has helpful leaflets, available from there or downloadable from www.familyrecords.gov.uk.

Chapter 7

Baptisms, Marriages and Burials

Parish registers

Until the civil registration of births, marriages and deaths was introduced in England and Wales in 1837, parish registers of the Church sacraments of baptism, marriage and burial were the only records of these life events. Parish registers have been in use since the 16th century (and continue today) and once you have exhausted the GRO indexes it is to these ancient ledgers that you will turn.

In 1538 Thomas Cromwell, Henry VIII's Vicar General, ordered every clergyman to keep records of all the baptisms, marriages and burials that he performed. Many of the very earliest of these lists, in flimsy registers or sometimes just on loose pieces of paper, have long been lost. The system did not work very satisfactorily anyway, and in 1597 ministers were told that they must use durable, parchment registers. They should have copied into these new books all the events that they had recorded since 1538 but, human nature being what it is, most only went back to 1558, when Queen Elizabeth I had come to the throne.

At the same time, ministers were ordered to send duplicate copies once a year to their bishop. These ***Bishops' Transcripts*** sometimes survive when the original registers have been lost and are a useful way of checking information. In some cases, there is information in the transcripts that does not appear in the registers and you should always look at these records if they exist. They will be found at record offices, usually on microfilm, alongside the registers. Some ministers continued to send them to their bishop until the 1870s or 1880s.

The turmoil of the Civil War and the Interregnum (1642-1660) affected the keeping of many church records. There may well be gaps in the registers in this period, or they may be poorly kept. In 1653 Oliver Cromwell took custody of the registers out of the hands of the parish clergy and gave them instead to 'able and honest' men who were to be elected annually and known as the 'Parish Register'. All marriages were ordered to take place before a magistrate instead of a minister. Baptism tailed off sharply. In 1660 when the monarchy was restored, an act legalised all marriages made since May 1642 and many parish registers show a great number of adult baptisms being performed over the next few years.

The format of the registers

If you first look at parish registers for an event that took place in the 1820s or 1830s, you will find them to be standardised, printed volumes, with baptisms, marriages and burials kept separately. As you go back in time, however, you will see that changes have taken place in the registers and the information recorded since the 16th century.

The early registers had no standard format and included baptisms, marriages and burials in one book. The parish minister (or his clerk) either mixed all events together, particularly in small parishes where there were few entries to make each year, or listed them, by year, with, for example, all baptisms together. It is worth spending a few minutes looking through a register when you first encounter it, to make sure that you understand the system the vicar used, as it can sometimes be easy to miss an entry if it is, perhaps, a baptism inserted in a series of burials.

After 1754 an important change took place following **Hardwicke's Marriage Act**: 'An Act for the better Preventing of Clandestine Marriages'. In a tightening up of the rules provoked by a rash of casual marriages and scandalous abductions, from 25th March in that year all marriages (except those of Quakers and Jews) had to be either preceded by the calling of banns or permitted by licence, and the ceremony had to take place in the parish where either the bride or groom lived; if either of them was under 21, the consent of a parent was necessary. Entries recording the marriage were to be kept separately in a specially printed book. This contained standard forms, in which had to be written the names of the couple, their signatures and those of the priest and the witnesses.

The calling of banns was also recorded and the **banns book** may have survived. The information can sometimes be useful – if, for instance, you know the home parish of one of the parties but not where the marriage took place, the banns book may give a clue in naming the home parish of the intended bride or groom. Banns books will be found at record offices,

'P' for Pauper - An act of 1694, raising money for a war against France, imposed taxes on register entries of baptisms, marriages and burials (as well as on bachelors and widowers). As paupers were exempt from paying the tax, a rash of pauperism broke out and you may find your ancestor has a 'P' beside their name in the register, indicating they were in receipt of poor relief from the parish.

Finding registers and transcripts

The original parish registers are, in most cases, deposited for safekeeping with the local record office, with the minister of the parish church retaining only those registers that are still in use.

In some very small parishes, where few baptisms, marriages or burials take place each year, a register may still be current that was started in the late 1800s, but in general you will only have to approach the minister if you wish to find an entry from the last half of the 20th century. He or she is entitled to charge you a standard fee for seeing the register and you will probably have to search it under supervision at the church.

You may find that your ancestor has illustrious companions in the churchyard – this was the funeral of Sir Robert Peel, former Prime Minister, at Drayton Bassett in 1850.

At the record office, most pre-1900 registers have been microfilmed or microfiched and you will rarely see the original books, although they can be produced if necessary. Obviously, the archivists' primary concern is to save wear and tear on these precious volumes. In any case, taking copies of entries from microform copies is easy and convenient.

Transcripts of registers, compiled probably in the 19th and 20th centuries, are often available at record offices and some family history societies have published sets of them for sale. If there is an index with the transcript, it will save you a great deal of time, but do check the index entry against the original and, if you cannot find the entry you want in the index, check the original anyway – it may have been missed or misread. There are also some transcripts available on the Internet; try searching under the parish name. Again, always check against the original when you can.

Indexes

The major problem with researching before 1837 is that ancestors who moved about from parish to parish may be extremely difficult to trace (and people certainly moved about the country with far greater fluidity than many historians would have us believe).

Apart from the indexes created by antiquarians and family historians when they made transcripts of the parish registers, there are several other finding aids including:

1. The International Genealogical Index (IGI)
2. Boyd's Marriage Index and other marriage indexes
3. The National Burial Index (NBI)
4. Projects by Family History Societies

The IGI is an enormous index of names, mostly baptisms, extracted from parish registers, nonconformist registers and bishops' transcripts. It has been compiled by the Genealogical Department of the Church of Latter-day Saints (otherwise known as the LDS, or Mormons) and the Church has generously made it, and much else, publicly and freely available. The IGI will be found in libraries and record offices, LDS Family

Surname	Forename	Date / Age	Location	
WARD	Ann	02/Dec/1838 60	Great Amwell	St John the Baptist
WARD	Ann	19/Sep/1839 9m	Wyddial	St Giles
WARD	Ann	02/Mar/1840 13	St Paul's Walden	All Saints
WARD	Ann	23/May/1841 60	Layston & Buntingf'd	St Bartholemew

Part of a printout from Hertfordshire Family History Society's Burial Index. (courtesy Hertfordshire FHS)

History Centres, Family History Societies, and on the Internet, free of charge, at www.familysearch.org.

The Index is, as its name says, international, but for the U.K. it is divided first into countries - England, Wales, Scotland, Ireland - and then into the pre-1974 counties. In 1974 county boundaries were redrawn and your ancestors may very well have been living in what is now the county next door. Surnames are listed alphabetically and are grouped to include possible name variants. Most of the entries are pre-1813 but certainly do not stop when civil registration began and you will find events there from as late as the 1870s.

The IGI was not, however, originally created for family historians and this explains some of its limitations and idiosyncracies. The entries consist mainly of births or baptisms, with many marriages but hardly any burials, and because the LDS allowed members of the Church to include private contributions, not all the information can be relied on. Not all parishes are included (you can easily check what is there by looking on the website, or at the Parish and Vital Records List on microfiche) and some counties are better covered than others. However, in this it is like every other index - the entry must be cross-checked with original sources before you can be sure of its provenance.

Never construct a family tree solely from the IGI! It is a finding aid only, although an invaluable one.

Boyd's Marriage Index, in 531 volumes, contains an astounding six or seven million marriages from the years 1538 to 1837, although this is sadly only up to about 15% of all English marriages in the period. It is divided by county, and is indexed by the names of both bride and groom, giving the year of marriage and the parish. Record offices may have a copy for their county. The original Index is held by the Society of Genealogists and much of it is now available on the www.britishorigins.com website.

There are also many other county marriage indexes, some of them created by individuals, others by family history societies or record offices themselves. Always ask the archive staff or local FHS what is available. A useful source for London in the late 18th and early 19th centuries, where it is notoriously easy to 'lose' ancestors, is the Pallot Marriage Index, which is available on CD-ROM and on Ancestry.com (pay per view).

The **National Burial Index** is a recent project organised by the Federation of Family History Societies to transcribe and make available in searchable form all burials in England and Wales. You can find further information on current coverage of the Index on www.ffhs.org.uk. County FHSs have sometimes produced their own indexes, with more information or covering a wider period.

Family History Societies have ongoing projects which very often include transcription or indexing of parish registers in their county. There are details of FHS addresses and websites at www.ffhs.org.uk.

Finding out more

Phillimore Atlas and Index of Parish Registers, Cecil Humphery-Smith, Phillimore, 3rd ed, 2003

An Introduction to Church Registers, Lilian Gibbens, FFHS, 1997

Bishops' Transcripts and Marriage Licences, Bonds and Allegations: A Guide to their Location and Indexes, Jeremy Gibson, FFHS, 5th ed, 2001

Palaeography for Family and Local Historians, Hilary Marshall, Phillimore, 2004

Online tutorial on reading old handwriting: www.nationalarchives.gov.uk/palaeography

Chapter 8

Nonconformist Ancestors

Many people will discover, perhaps to their surprise, that their ancestors did not worship in the Church of England (except under protest). The possibility that they were nonconformists should always be borne in mind, particularly if an individual seems to have disappeared from the church records.

'Nonconformist' generally refers to those groups which, since the 17th century, have broken away from the Church of England to worship in their own congregations. They have a complicated history, but the main groups are:

Quakers, or Society of Friends. Founded in the mid 1600s. Their records are often informative, particularly for marriages, which were subject to keen scrutiny as marriage with a non-Quaker would lead to expulsion. Births, rather than baptisms, are recorded, and many Quaker meeting houses had their own burial grounds.

Baptists. Founded 1611 and split by 1633 into Particular Baptists and General Baptists; reunited in 1891. Registers of adult baptism.

Presbyterians/Unitarians and Congregationalists/Independents. Dissenting groups since the 17th century, with thousands of chapels throughout England and Wales. In 1972 the Presbyterians and Congregationalists joined to form the United Reformed Church.

Methodists. Formed in the 1730s within the Church of England, and broke away in the late 18th century under the influence of John Wesley and George Whitfield (who formed the Countess of Huntingdon's Connexion). Separate registers therefore only from the 1790s at the earliest. In the 1800s the evangelical revival in working class and rural areas led to the splitting off of the Primitive Methodists and other groups (most of the Methodist churches were reunited in 1932).

The Quaker funeral of Mrs John Bright in 1878 at Rochdale. The Illustrated London News *reported that: 'The scene differed only from an ordinary largely-attended funeral by the utter absence of ceremonial parade, and of any sort of ecclesiastical attire, which distinguishes this sober, steadfast, God-fearing community of old-fashioned English Puritans.'*

When you are just beginning your research, nonconformity is unlikely to cause any problems, as all births, marriages and deaths will appear in the civil registration system since 1837.

Once you reach the early 19th century, however, and start to consult parish registers, it is helpful to know at least something of the history of nonconformity and its records since Henry VIII broke from the Roman Catholic Church, leading eventually to the establishment of the Church of England.

- **1662 Act of Uniformity** A sign of increased hostility towards dissenters, when nonconforming ministers were expelled from their parishes. Their followers at this early period had no option but to be baptised, married and buried in the parish church, and are therefore recorded in the parish registers.
- **1689 Toleration Act** An easing of restrictions as long as an oath of loyalty was sworn, allowing dissenters to have their own clergy, teachers and places of worship. So there may be separate registers from then on (though burials are likely to be still in the parish churchyard as few chapels had their own burial ground).
- **1753 Hardwicke's Marriage Act** Made it illegal to contract a marriage by simply making a declaration before witnesses (exempting

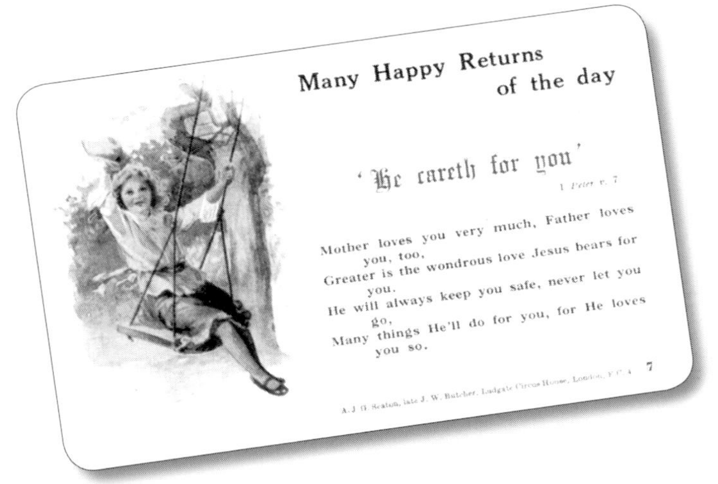

Clues to a nonconformist background can come from surprising sources. The back of this birthday postcard says 'With love from the Chilwell Road Methodist Sunday School'.

Quakers and Jews). Nonconformists therefore had to marry in the parish church.

- **1836 Marriage Act** Allowed nonconformist chapels and churches to apply for a licence to perform marriages, although as there was a fee, smaller congregations could not afford to do so. The following year, 1837, brought the possibility of marriage in a register office, which many nonconformists preferred to the parish church.
- **1850s onwards** With the opening of private and municipal cemeteries, nonconformists had the option not to be buried in the parish churchyard.

In 1837 nonconformist registers should have been deposited with the Registrar General, and those that were received are held by The National Archives. They have been microfilmed and copies will be found at county record offices, which will be able to advise on other nonconformist records for the area. Remember that congregations were not based upon the parish and could cross county boundaries, depending on the circuit of a travelling minister. Some nonconformist entries are included in the

International Genealogical Index (IGI). The different groups also have their own specialised archives.

Although not nonconformists in the usual sense, there are two other important religious groups which stood apart from the Anglican church:

Roman Catholics

Catholics did not share in the general spread of religious toleration of the later 17th century and freedom to worship was restricted until the 1829 Catholic Emancipation Act. Some registers have been published, some remain with the churches and some are deposited in record offices.

Jews

Records are usually held by the synagogue, as Jewish congregations were not required to deposit their registers with the Registrar General in 1837. *The Jewish Year Book* lists synagogues and Jewish cemeteries.

Finding out more

Tracing Nonconformist Ancestors, Michael Gandy, TNA, 2001

My Ancestors were Baptists, Geoffrey R. Breed, Society of Genealogists (SoG), 4th ed, 2002

My Ancestors were Congregationalists in England and Wales, David J. H. Clifford, SoG, 2nd ed, 1997

My Ancestors were English Presbyterians/Unitarians, Alan Ruston, SoG, 2nd ed, 2001

My Ancestors were Quakers, E. H. Milligan & M. J. Thomas, SoG, 3rd ed, 2005

Basic Facts about Methodist Records for Family Historians, Richard Ratcliffe, FFHS, 2005

Tracing Your Catholic Ancestors, Michael Gandy, TNA, 2001

Jewish Ancestors? A Beginner's Guide to Jewish Genealogy in Great Britain, Rosemary Wenzerul, Jewish Genealogical Society of Great Britain, 2001

For links to the Quaker, Catholic and Jewish family history societies, visit www.ffhs.org.uk

Chapter 9

The Records of the Poor

'Resolve not to be poor', said Dr Johnson, and our ancestors would certainly have agreed. There can be few families that have not been touched by poverty in some way or other over the centuries, either receiving help or as long-suffering ratepayers. As a family historian, you will find that the records created since the 16th century will throw light upon the lives of even the humblest of your ancestors.

The acceptance that the able-bodied should take responsibility for the support of those who fell into hardship through no fault of their own (the 'deserving' poor) battled with the resentment of ratepayers at having to pay to relieve migrant workers and those who would not work to help themselves (the 'undeserving' poor) from Tudor times right through to the 20th century, if not to the present day.

Records created by the working of the Poor Laws are a very useful source for family historians. What is referred to as the 'Poor Law' is a general term for the many acts that were passed to control and direct poverty relief from the 16th century until the creation of the Welfare State in 1948. It can be divided into:

(i) The Old Poor Law to 1834

(ii) The New Poor Law from 1834

(iii) Public Assistance from 1930 to 1948

The **Old Poor Law** is a convenient term to describe a series of laws that were consolidated in 1598 and 1601. It was administered by the parish, through Overseers of the Poor, and based on compulsory contributions by the better-off as poor rates. This system was in place for over 200 years and elements of the Old Poor Law, such as settlement and the workhouse, continued under the New Poor Law.

The **New Poor Law** came into operation in 1834, and was an effort to

The 'undeserving' poor were frequently accused of spending all their money on drink. The temperance movement grew rapidly from the 1850s.

cope with the rising population and the distressing effects of economic hardship in the early decades of the 19th century. The country was divided into Unions, by grouping parishes together (although not always following parish or county boundaries), and Guardians of the Poor were elected to act in committee to relieve the poor. The system was still based upon local poor rates.

The records that the poor law system created, which will be found at county record offices, included:

- **overseers' account books**, which may detail payments to named individuals for food, clothing, nursing, burial, etc. Churchwardens' accounts may also contain some information relating to poor relief.

  Later, Boards of Guardians took over this function and details may be found in the minutes of their meetings.

- **parish rates books**, which could be of great help in tracking individuals who were not themselves poor but who had to pay local rates.

- **settlement certificates**. First introduced by an act of 1662, these certificates were the initial ammunition in a battle between the ratepayers and the poor that went on for centuries. 'Settlement' simply meant the right of an individual or family to be able to claim to 'belong' to a particular parish. If they fell sick or needed help (became 'chargeable') when they were travelling or living elsewhere, they could be sent back to their home parish, where they would be looked after. A settlement certificate was the piece of paper that identified that home parish, a kind of passport for the poor. Only migrant workers had to hold them at first, but from 1697 anyone who looked likely to fall under the Poor Laws had to have a certificate to move into, or stay in, a new parish. The actual certificate was signed by the overseers of the poor, the churchwardens and two witnesses, before two magistrates.

The background to settlement is quite complicated and over hundreds of years the conditions changed but, in general, if a person was born in a parish, or served an apprenticeship there, or lived there for over a year without needing financial help they would be welcome to stay and the parish would take responsibility for them if they fell on hard times (as they would, also, if they were actually paying local rates).

If your ancestor became ill or destitute while living away from his or her parish of settlement, a **settlement examination** took place before a magistrate. Where they survive, these documents can provide a great deal of useful information for family history, being almost a potted biography. The examination could lead to the issue of a **removal order**, authorising the local overseers to send your ancestor back to where he or she came from.

The poor preferred to find what charity they could, even in a soup kitchen, rather than enter the workhouse.

- **bastardy bonds, bastardy examinations**. Illegitimate children were unwelcome if they became a charge on the parish, so great efforts were made to track down the erring father.
- **workhouse records**. The first workhouses (literally to provide work for the able-bodied poor) were built in the 16th century, but during the 18th century parishes were allowed to club together to provide shelter for the old, the sick and the destitute. You will rarely be able to find records for these earlier workhouses, but after 1834 it should be easier. From that year the workhouse became the loathed institution that still had the power to strike fear into the hearts of the poor in the 20th century, deliberately so as it was meant to discourage people from applying for poor relief. Registers of births and deaths, admissions and discharges are deposited at the local record office. Workhouse inmates are listed in the census returns.

From 1930 until the Welfare State came into existence in 1948 there was a period when poor relief was the responsibility of county and county borough councils, under the Ministry of Health. This was a time of great economic depression, when millions of people suffered hardship and many families who would normally have kept their heads above water had to swallow their pride and apply for assistance. The old workhouses were taken over and often renamed as hospitals, but without removing that Victorian bleak and uncaring image.

For this period, look for the records of the Public Assistance Committee and the Area Guardians Committee; they may contain details relating to claimants for poor relief, including age, address, the names of relatives, date of death and details of burial – all things you may not be able to find anywhere else.

Finding out more

An Introduction to Poor Law Documents before 1834, Anne Cole, FFHS, 2nd ed, 2000

Using Poor Law Records, Simon Fowler, TNA, 2001

The Parish Chest, William Tate, Phillimore, 3rd ed, 1974

Chapter 10
Wills

Wills were not just written by the rich and powerful. Thousands of wills survive in the archives that can throw light on the lives, possessions and family relationships of ordinary people. It is always worth checking if a member of your family left a will, however poor you think they may have been.

The object of making a will has not changed over the centuries. Written authority is given to named executors to divide up the deceased's property as he or she wished. In the distant past, a will was concerned only with disposal of land, and personal property was dealt with in a 'testament', but that distinction has been blurred for a long time and, except in very early wills, a 'last will and testament' relates to all of a person's property.

A will is usually not valid unless it is made in writing, and signed in the presence of two witnesses, who also sign the document. The only exceptions to this general rule are servicemen on active service or mariners, who can make a valid will on any scrap of paper, unwitnessed (a holograph will) or even verbally before witnesses (a nuncupative will). The latter was generally legal prior to 1838.

The 'last will and testament' might be completed on the deathbed, or it could have been written some time before the death.

The information you can find in a will obviously varies according to the individuals involved. However, you may discover the deceased's address and occupation, names and addresses of family members, family relationships (even sometimes previously unknown connections, such as illegitimate children), names and addresses of the executors, who may be friends or business colleagues of the deceased, daughters' married names, the value of the estate and perhaps details of property and other possessions and, in addition, charitable bequests may reveal beliefs or interests that could be of help in tracing your ancestor's past life, and a burial (or cremation) place may be specified.

If someone dies intestate in England and Wales (that is, without leaving a will), or if the will is invalid for any reason, a relative or other interested party can apply for **Letters of Administration** (also known as admin or admons) to allow them to manage the estate. Letters of administration give less information, but can still be useful, giving you the date of death, names and addresses and the estimated worth of the estate.

Note all the names and details you come across in a will – someone who you think is unrelated may turn out to be a hitherto unknown member of the family.

Don't jump to conclusions. If a son or daughter is left out of the bequests, it may be because the deceased made other arrangements during his or her lifetime (such as leaving the estate to the eldest son), rather than evidence of a rift in the family. Married daughters may have had money or property settled on them when they married, and no other provision will be made for them when their father dies.

Wills are only preserved in the archives because they have gone through the process of probate. It is perfectly possible that your family sorted things out between themselves when a relative died and therefore never needed to seek official sanction. An ancestor you thought was wealthy enough to warrant a will may not therefore appear in the probate records for that reason. On the other hand, you may find ancestors in the records that you would never have expected. Once a will has gone through probate it is open to anyone to request to see it, through the channels detailed below (things worked slightly differently in Scotland – see Chapter 14.)

Where to find modern wills (from 1858 onwards)

You need to be aware that 1858 is a key year for research into ancestors' wills in England and Wales. Before that year, the grant of probate was the responsibility of a wide range of Church courts. After 12th January 1858, all wills were brought under the control of a centralised civil system of probate registries, in a system that, in essence, continues today.

All wills, admons, etc., proved in the Court of Probate since 1858 are held at the Principal Probate Registry, First Avenue House, 42-49 High Holborn, London WC1 6NP (telephone: 020 7947 6000).

A soldier's will could be written without the usual safeguards of witnesses etc 'on the eve of battle' or on active service. A form for a will was included in every soldier's Service & Pay Book.

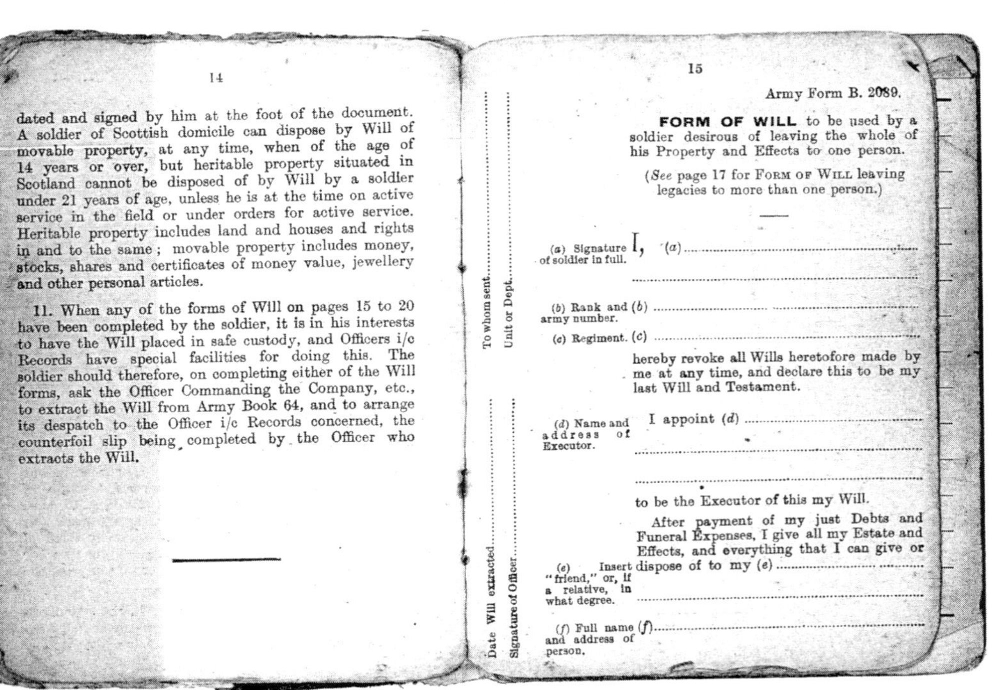

14

dated and signed by him at the foot of the document. A soldier of Scottish domicile can dispose by Will of movable property, at any time, when of the age of 14 years or over, but heritable property situated in Scotland cannot be disposed of by Will by a soldier under 21 years of age, unless he is at the time on active service in the field or under orders for active service. Heritable property includes land and houses and rights in and to the same; movable property includes money, stocks, shares and certificates of money value, jewellery and other personal articles.

11. When any of the forms of Will on pages 15 to 20 have been completed by the soldier, it is in his interests to have the Will placed in safe custody, and Officers i/c Records have special facilities for doing this. The soldier should therefore, on completing either of the Will forms, ask the Officer Commanding the Company, etc., to extract the Will from Army Book 64, and to arrange its despatch to the Officer i/c Records concerned, the counterfoil slip being completed by the Officer who extracts the Will.

To whom sent..................

Unit or Dept..................

Date Will extracted..................

Signature of Officer..................

15

Army Form B. 2089.

FORM OF WILL to be used by a soldier desirous of leaving the whole of his Property and Effects to one person.

(*See* page 17 for FORM OF WILL leaving legacies to more than one person.)

(*a*) Signature of soldier in full. I, (*a*) ....

(*b*) Rank and army number. (*b*) ....

(*c*) Regiment. (*c*) ....

hereby revoke all Wills heretofore made by me at any time, and declare this to be my last Will and Testament.

(*d*) Name and address of Executor. I appoint (*d*) ....

to be the Executor of this my Will.

After payment of my just Debts and Funeral Expenses, I give all my Estate and Effects, and everything that I can give or dispose of to my (*e*) ....

(*e*) Insert "friend," or, if a relative, in what degree.

(*f*) Full name and address of person. (*f*) ....

Annual indexes (known as the National Probate Calendar) have been published every year since 1858 by the Principal Probate Registry.These include every will and administration proved in Great Britain and, in the past, its dependent territories, such as South Africa or the West Indies. The indexes will give you names, addresses, date of death, occupation, and the value of the estate. You can see the indexes on microfiche at archives around the country – your local county record office will have copies – and they are held at The National Archives, the Family Records Centre, the Society of Genealogists and the Guildhall Library in London.

Local probate registries (some 40 in number) may have records of more modern date, but applications for searches there must be made in person. Information on probate registries, and on post-1858 probate records in general, is available at www.hmcourts-service.gov.uk

When you are searching the indexes, do not give up if you find nothing in the year you know that your ancestor died. Wills are sometimes not proved until several years after a death.

Once you have found an entry in the indexes for the will you want, you can either go to First Avenue House in person to see it, or write for a copy to Postal Searches and Copies Department, The Probate Registry, First Floor, Castle Chambers, Clifford Street, York YO1 9RG (you can ask them to do a search of the indexes for you, if you want). Make sure you have noted down all the relevant information from the index entry.There is a fee for searches and for providing copies of wills.

Until the Married Women's Property Act of 1882, a married woman could not make a will without her husband's consent, no matter what property or wealth she may have brought to a marriage. However, single women and widows could, and did, make wills, and it is always worth widening your searches to include all members of a family.

Wills proved before 1858

Before 1858, wills were proved only in Church courts. Unfortunately, the organisation of these courts can be confusing and the decision as to which court had jurisdiction depended on the value and whereabouts of an estate, making the search for an older will a little more difficult. In recent years, however, indexing and online availability have transformed the process.

When a person died, their will was taken to the appropriate Church court to be registered. This involved copying the will into a register book, which may mean that the copy has survived to the present day whereas the loose-leaf original has long since disappeared. The copy may be easier to read too, although you should be prepared to have to decipher 'old' handwriting and perhaps Latin, too.

The great majority of wills were proved by local Church courts. Many of these had a very restricted local authority – the middling-sized county of Hertfordshire, for instance, had eight ecclesiastical courts with different jurisdictions. The best person to advise you in your search is the county archivist. Enlist the help of the staff in the county records office, as they will be able to advise you if, for instance, the property owned by your ancestor was divided between several parishes, or even counties. Many record offices have locally-produced indexes to the records they hold. Maps showing ecclesiastical jurisdictions in all counties are in the *Phillimore Atlas and Index of Parish Registers* (3rd ed, 2003).

At the top of the Church hierarchy were the two Archbishops' courts, and it would be here that your ancestor's will was proved if he (or she) held property in more than one diocese. The Prerogative Court of York (PCY) dealt with wills proved in York, Durham, Northumberland, Westmorland, Cumberland, Lancashire, Cheshire, Nottinghamshire and the Isle of Man. The records are held at the Borthwick Institute of Historical Research, University of York, Heslington, York YO10 5DD (telephone: 01904 321166; www.york.ac.uk/inst/bihr). There are some probate indexes on www.britishorigins.com.

The highest probate court, however, was the Prerogative Court of Canterbury (PCC). Originally only estates worth more than £5 (£10 in London) were dealt with by the PCC, but although this was a lot of money in medieval times, by the 19th century a huge number of people could have their wills proved in the PCC. Fashion played its part too, as it was far more prestigious to have a will proved in London or York than in a small provincial court. The system, too, was complicated and, as the centuries went by, more and more people became eligible for the Archbishops' courts. There are, for instance, over 6,000 wills of men who died at sea amongst the PCC records.

The PCC wills are now available online from The National Archives and

This is the last Will and Testament of me Frederick Orchin of the Coach and Horses Beer House situate in Gloucester Road Croydon Common in the parish of Croydon County of Surrey I give devise and bequeath as follows There are two freehold messuages situate and being No 1 and 2 called Melton Cottages Hanbey Road Thornton Heath in the said parish of Croydon also the Beer House Stock in trade fixtures all furniture and effects in fact everything I may be possessed of or entitled to at the time of my decease I desire to be disposed of by my Executor hereinafter named and the proceeds to be equally divided between my Children then living share and share alike And I hereby nominate and appoint John Marshall Harris Hatter of 27a High Street in the parish of Croydon sole Executor and Trustee of this my last will and testament revoking all other wills and bequests and declare this and this only to be my last will and testament In witness whereof I have set my hand this ninth day of November in the year of our Lord One thousand eight hundred and seventy five — Frederick Orchin — Signed and pronounced by the said testator as his last will and testament in presence of us present at the same time who at his request and in his presence and presence of each other have subscribed our names as witnesses thereto — James Henry Barker, Croydon — David Lawn, South Norwood.

Part of a copy of the will of Frederick Orchin 'of the Coach and Horses Beer House in Gloucester Road Croydon Common', proved on 1st July 1876.

it is well worthwhile seeing if your ancestor's will may have been proved there: see www.nationalarchives.gov.uk/documentsonline. There is a fee to download images of the will, but the site is fully searchable and very useful. You can also see images of the wills of William Shakespeare, Admiral Nelson or Jane Austen, amongst others, if you want a break from the family!

Inventories

An inventory of your ancestor's possessions may exist, which can be a wonderful way to help to build a picture of his or her life and work.

From 1529 to 1782 the personal estate of a deceased person (i.e. not real estate) might be inventoried and valued by two or more appraisors appointed by the court. It was intended to prevent disputes over the division of property after the will had been proved or letters of administration granted. If you are lucky, you may find an inventory that describes, room by room, the possessions that your ancestor held dear during his life, and the tools of his trade, or his livestock.

Thousands of these inventories survive, some of them held at local record offices, together with the will or admon. Others are lodged at The National Archives with the PCC papers (classes PROB 2,3,4 and 5). They are usually filed with the probate papers, but are sometimes kept separately with the records of the relevant ecclesiastical court.

Death Duty Registers

Using the Death Duty Registers can be a shortcut to finding the ecclesiastical court in which your ancestor's will was proved, or to a date of death.

First imposed in 1780, death duty (or legacy duty, probate duty, or estate duty) was consistently imposed on the estate of the deceased from 1796 onwards; in 1975, it became Capital Transfer Tax. The value of the estate that fell under this tax and the people affected have varied over the centuries, but if your ancestor appears in the records you may find out the actual worth of their estate and what happened to it, the date of death, the beneficiaries and the next of kin. As the records were open to amendment for 50 years after they were first created, there may also be information about events that happened years after the death of the named ancestor.

The indexed records are held at The National Archives and the Family Records Centre (on microfilm) and some are available online (currently 1796 to 1811) at www.nationalarchives.gov.uk.

Finding out more

Basic Facts About Using Wills After 1858 and First Avenue House, Audrey Collins, FFHS, 1998

Probate Jurisdictions: Where to Look for Wills, Jeremy Gibson and Else Churchill, FFHS, 5th ed., 2002

Using Wills, Karen Grannum, TNA, 2000

Wills and Other Probate Records: A Practical Guide to Researching Your Ancestors' Last Documents, Karen Grannum & Nigel Taylor, TNA, 2004

Chapter 11

Military Ancestors

The chances are that members of your family fought in the First World War (1914-1918) or Second World War (1939-1945). You might decide to research these individuals in depth. If so, there are many books, websites and research aids to help you locate the records and fill in the historical background.

A great deal of the archive material that you will need is held at The National Archives. However, there are two things you would be well advised to do before anything else, simply because they may save you a great deal of wasted time and effort, not to mention money. Talk to your family, and hunt out every bit of memorabilia that the family possesses. Every small detail will be helpful, even if it only helps you to differentiate between two men or women of the same name in the official records.

Regimental badges may help to identify a soldier's unit.

To use the archives successfully you need to know:

1. The service he or she was in – Navy, Army, Air Force?
2. Whether he or she was an 'other rank' or an officer.
3. The period of time he or she served (a rough idea will do at the start).
4. The unit, regiment or ship in which he or she served (again, a useful aid if you can find it easily, although people often transferred between units or ships during their service).

Museums can be great places to absorb the background information that will help you to bring your researches to life. They may not necessarily have documentary sources, but their collections and exhibits are usually of an extremely high standard.

- www.armymuseums.org.uk has links to regimental museums and helpful advice on tracing individuals
- www.royal-navy.mod.uk/static/pages/1935.html has links to Royal Navy museums
- www.rafmuseum.org.uk gives tips on tracing RAF servicemen and women
- www.iwm.org.uk is the website of the Imperial War Museum, which has information on research

There is a vast amount of information available for anyone trying to trace their family members' wartime service in depth, and a list of useful books that will introduce you to the sometimes complicated archives is given at the end of this chapter. In the limited space here, it is possible only to give an idea of the kind of records you can consult, but there are two sources you can investigate immediately using the Internet. Researching Second

Researching the background of a soldier's life in the services – such as understanding the amount of kit he had to carry with him – can make a fascinating addition to the official documents.

While the First World War went on, servicemen's graves could only be tended superficially. After the war the Commonwealth War Graves Commission took over responsibility for the memorials and graves of the fallen.

World War service can be more difficult as the papers for servicemen and women have not been released to The National Archives. They are still retained by the relevant Service department, with restrictions on their availability.

The Debt of Honour database of the Commonwealth War Graves Commission (CWGC)

If the relative you are researching died in the services during either of the two world wars, his or her death and burial place (or place of commemoration) will have been recorded by the CWGC. The Commission also maintains a roll of honour for over 66,000 civilians who died as a result of enemy action in the Second World War, mainly in air raids.

The CWGC was founded during the First World War and takes responsibility for caring for the graves of fallen servicemen and women in over 2,000 sites in 150 countries around the world, taking as their parameters the periods of August 1914 to August 1921 and September 1939 to December 1947.

The familiar white CWGC stone raised over each grave, with no distinction between ranks, races or creeds, bears the name of the serviceman or woman, a regimental or unit badge (or a national symbol, such as a maple leaf for a Canadian soldier), a religious symbol selected by the family, and a personal inscription of up to four lines.

The CWGC also maintains memorials for those with no known grave, such as the Menin Gate at Ypres, where over 53,000 names are inscribed.

In the last few years, the CWGC has computerised its vast records and created a searchable database online – they deal with over 250,000 enquiries a month. The Debt of Honour database at www.cwgc.org is easy to use and very efficient, or write to them at 2 Marlow Road, Maidenhead, Berks SL6 7DX; telephone: 01628 634221 (there may be a small charge for postal enquiries).The CWGC will then be able to provide you with the place of burial or commemoration, date of death, rank, unit, and perhaps the next of kin and home address.

The National Archives' online database at www.nationalarchives.gov.uk/documentsonline/

There are several useful aids available online which will shed light on First World War service. You can search and download (for a fee) the following, for instance:

- the Medal Rolls Index, or Medal Index Cards – 5.5 million medal cards, containing information about individuals used to assess their medal entitlement at the end of the First World War. Each gives the rank and any changes, units served in, and the first operational theatre they entered (e.g. France and Belgium). Directions are given on how to make a search and on how to interpret the information and abbreviations found.
- the service registers of more than 500,000 seamen who joined the Royal Navy between 1853 and 1923 (covering the periods of the Crimean, Boer and First World Wars). The records, from the ADM 188 series, give name, age, place of birth, service history and ships served on, plus (after 1873) a physical description.

Medals

The three most common First World War campaign medals are the 1914 Star (or the 1914-1915 Star), the British War Medal and the Victory Medal. These were so familiar after the war that they were cheerfully known as 'Pip, Squeak and Wilfred' after a trio of cartoon characters, so these are likely to turn up quite regularly in homes all over the country.

A tip is to look at the back or the rim of the medal, where you should find the name, rank and serial number of the man to whom they were awarded engraved, plus his regiment or ship – a very useful addition to your information. Identifying medals, and the ribbons and clasps that may be with them, can be done quite easily with the help of the books listed below.

For the Second World War, the 1939-45 Star was given to all who saw active service. Other medals commemorated different campaigns, such as the Burma Star, the Italy Star, the Atlantic Star and so on. The Defence Medal or 1939-45 War Medal was awarded to anyone, including civilians, who served only in Britain.

Finding out more

Tracing Your First World War Ancestors, Simon Fowler, Countryside Books, 2003

Identifying Your World War One Soldier from Badges and Photographs, Iain Swinnerton, FFHS, 2001

Tracing Your Second World War Ancestors, Simon Fowler, Countryside Books, 2006

British Campaign Medals 1815-1914; *British Campaign Medals 1914-2000; British Gallantry Medals 1855-2000*, all by Peter Duckers (Shire Books, 2000/2001)

Medals: The Researcher's Companion, William Spencer, The National Archives, 2006

www.nationalarchives.gov.uk/documentsonline/medals.asp

www.medals.org.uk

www.findmypast.com for rolls of honour, army births, marriages and deaths etc.

Chapter 12

Other Archive Sources

There are many other sources that family historians may find useful, which are impossible to cover in the space available here. Widen your search once you have mastered the basics of family history, and spend some time discovering what can be found at your local record office, as well as amongst the huge resources at the national repositories.

School records

Log books and admissions registers may reveal details of your ancestor's childhood. Many records are deposited at County Record Offices (CROs) although there may be restrictions on viewing more recent documents. Independent schools may have retained their records and even employ their own archivist; there is also material relating to the public schools at the Society of Genealogists. Look also for school registers, histories, magazines and yearbooks. University rolls have been published.

Electoral registers and poll books

Electoral registers (lists of people entitled to vote at elections) can be used to locate families and track movement from place to place. They were first published in 1832 and then appeared annually, with a few exceptions. Poll books date back to the 17th century and record how people voted before the introduction of the secret ballot in 1872.

Tax returns

Government taxation has created records that in some cases go back to medieval times.These could include lay subsidies (12th to 17th centuries), poll tax (14th and 17th centuries), hearth tax (1662-1689), window and house tax (17th and 18th centuries), and land tax (from 1692). In 1910 the Inland Revenue surveyed all land for a proposed tax, producing maps and valuation books that list owners, occupiers and property. There are also local taxes, such as the parish rate assessment.

Manorial records

If your ancestor lived on a manorial estate, their lives may have been ruled by the manor court. Courts were still being held in some places well into the 20th century. Changes in property holdings may give details of family relationships, while tenants were also brought before the court for misdemeanours or if they needed help to settle a local quarrel.

Court records

From the 14th to the 19th centuries magistrates (Justices of the Peace, or JPs), sitting in Quarter Sessions, dealt not only with criminal cases but also with many local administrative functions that later came under the control of local councils. People's names appear in the Quarter Sessions records for many reasons, from applying for a licence to carry on a trade to answering for failing to maintain the highway. JPs also had many responsibilities under the Poor Laws, e.g. *Hertford Quarter Sessions Book; Vol 9; 14 April 1729: 'Order that the overseers of Braughin shall sell the goods of Francis Bembridge, who has run away and left his two children, Mary, aged eight, and Margaret, aged four, chargeable to the parish.'* There then follows a full inventory of all Francis Bembridge's possessions. Unfortunately, indexes are not always available, as happens with the records of ecclesiastical courts, which also have a huge amount of information within them but which can be impenetrable if you do not have a clear idea of what you are looking for.

There is a vast collection of other legal records at The National Archives, including those of the Court of Chancery. The Bernau Index, held by the Society of Genealogists, is a good starting point for these important records, particularly for the 18th century. On www.oldbaileyonline.com, court cases 1674-1834 (currently) have been indexed by name.

Apprenticeship records

To be able to carry on a trade, young men and women needed to have served an apprenticeship, usually of seven years. An indenture would be drawn up and signed by their parent or guardian (who might be the parish overseer) and by the master who took them on. When the apprenticeship was complete, it qualified them to become a freeman of the city or borough. A tax imposed in 1710 meant that registers of apprenticeships were maintained nationally for about the next 100 years and these records are held at The National Archives. Some have been published: *'DUROY, Mary, of St George ye Martyr: to Eliz. Hempfield, of St George ye Martyr, Mantua Maker: 20 Apr. 1730'* is one example from *Surrey Apprenticeships 1711-1731* published by the Surrey Record Society in 1929.

Until about 1750, the information included the father's or mother's name, which could be of great help in tracing a family. Not all apprenticeships were recorded, however, though it is still worth looking to see if your ancestor appears here (there is a partial index at the Society of Genealogists and the Guildhall Library). Many apprenticeships were informal agreements between local individuals and the papers will have disappeared long ago, but it is worth looking at local record offices, and the Society of Genealogists has a large collection of apprenticeship records of all types.

Finding out more

Basic facts about using education records, Colin Chapman, FFHS, 1999

Poll books c1696-1872: a directory to holdings in Great Britain, Jeremy Gibson & Colin Rogers, FFHS, 2002

Electoral registers since 1832, Jeremy Gibson & Colin Rogers, FFHS, 2002

Land and Window Tax Assessments, Jeremy Gibson, Mervyn Medlycott & Dennis Mills, FFHS, 2nd ed, 2004

Using Manorial Records, Mary Ellis, PRO, 1994

My Ancestors were Manorial Tenants, Peter Park, Society of Genealogists, 2002

Sex, Sin and Probate: Ecclesiastical Courts, Officials and Records, Colin Chapman, Lochin Publishing, 2nd ed, 1997.

The National Archives series of Research Guides.

How to Use the Bernau Index, Hilary Sharpe, SoG 2nd ed, 2000

My Ancestors were Freemen of the City of London, Vivienne E. Aldous, Society of Genealogists, 1999.

London Apprentices series, Cliff Webb, Society of Genealogists, various dates

Chapter 13

Outside the Archives

There is more to family history than simply collecting names and dates. As you begin to create your family tree, you will want to know what your ancestors did for a living, what kind of home life they had, in what surroundings they grew up and lived their adult lives, and what was going on in the world around them. History becomes doubly fascinating when you know that someone in your own family was alive at the time of great events.

Bringing your ancestors to life means researching the times in which they lived. Here are a few suggestions for ways to fill in the background:

Local histories

The boundaries between family history and local history are blurred and you will want to find out all you can about the history of the locality, the kinds of jobs done by the people who lived there, the way they lived and what events touched their lives. County Record Offices (CROs) and libraries are the best places to track down local histories, some of which may have been published only in very small quantities. Online, try putting the name of the parish into a good search engine - many places now have their own websites and some of these are very useful indeed.

Newspapers

These are a great source of information you will find nowhere else, and have the advantage that you can see for yourself what issues and events were important to the people of the time. They are also great for time-wasting, as you are sure to be sidetracked into reading all the advertisements and court reports! Unfortunately, very few are indexed (which would be a truly mammoth task, but your CRO should know if there is anything for your area) so it is to a great extent sheer luck that you will find anything relating directly to your ancestors. An exception might be if they were involved in a court case, or there was a sudden death in the family, when there may be a report of the coroner's court.

Local histories will tell you about events that may have affected your ancestors' lives, such as the Lancashire cotton factory riots in 1878, when Colonel Raynsford Jackson's house at Blackburn was burned by the rioters. (Illustrated London News, *25th May 1878)*

CROs usually have excellent archives of local newspapers going back to the early 1800s. The British Library Newspaper Collection (see Appendix) lists over 52,000 newspaper and periodical titles in their catalogue, dating from 1801 to the present day; you can easily search the catalogue on their website at www.bl.uk/collections/history.html (simply put the county name into the Search box and a full list of all newspapers held, and their dates, will be produced).

Directories

Directories can be a useful way of checking on addresses.They are also full of information about local services, such as the school or the workhouse. County directories have been printed since the early 1800s, though later ones give more detailed information, street by street. Kelly's is probably the most famous name but there are many more publishers, some very local. The directories are wonderful sources of advertisements for local businesses. Libraries often carry a stock of directories for their area, as do CROs; in London, the Society of Genealogists and the Guildhall Library have a wide range on open shelves. An increasing number have been published on CD-ROM by, for instance, Archive-CD Books. Look also at www.historicaldirectories.org which was set up by the University of Leicester and provides a searchable database of selected 19th-century directories.

Museums

Discover what is in your area by checking with the local authority (all have websites nowadays), the CRO or library. Or you can find a listing of over 3,500 museums and galleries all over the country, with contact details, at www.24hourmuseum.org.uk.

Occupations

You can find out what your ancestor did for a living from civil registration certificates and census returns, as well as from other documents such as wills. Finding out more about that occupation can be an absorbing task and is essential if you are to begin to flesh out the bare bones of genealogy. There are many books and websites that can help you (particularly with the interpretation of unfamiliar names for old occupations); www.genuki.org.uk/big/Occupations.html has a very useful listing of books and links to websites for both general occupational queries and specific industries and trades.

An Introduction to Occupations: A Preliminary List, Joyce Culling, FFHS, 2nd ed, 1999

A Dictionary of Old Trades, Titles and Occupations, Colin Waters, Countryside Books, 2nd ed, 2002

Occupational Sources for Genealogists: A Bibliography, Stuart A. Raymond, FFHS, 1996

Maps

Comparing a modern map with one printed even 50 years ago can be amazing. Road building, the loss of so many railway branch lines in the 1960s, and the spread of our ever-expanding towns and villages have

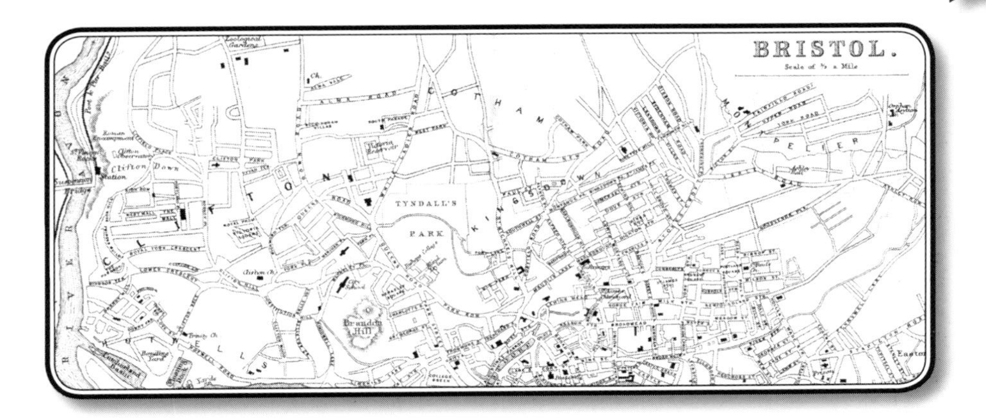

Part of a street map of Bristol included in Black's 'Picturesque Tourist of England' in 1874.

all affected how the landscape we see today differs from that known by our grandparents, or even our parents. Compare today's map with one printed 100 years ago or more, and the differences are even more remarkable.

There are several ways to get hold of copies of older, Victorian maps. Ordnance Survey maps from the original first editions have been reprinted by David & Charles (Maps Direct, Brunel House, Forde Close, Newton Abbot TQ12 2DW; telephone: 0870 9908222). Some of the OS First Series maps can also be found online at www.old-maps.co.uk. Alan Godfrey has republished large-scale OS maps from the late 1800s and early 1900s (mainly urban areas), as well as the one-inch to the mile maps, and the full list can be found at www.alangodfreymaps.co.uk (or write to Alan Godfrey Maps, Prospect Business Park, Leadgate, Consett DH8 7PW; telephone: 01207 583388). CROs and local studies departments in major libraries, will have copies of the old OS maps for their area.

Tithe maps

When you get back to the 1830s or 1840s, you may also want to look at tithe maps for a particular village. At that time the ancient tithe payments to the clergy (a tenth of all produce) were commuted into a cash sum, so all the land had to be surveyed and recorded to find out who owned or used it and would therefore be liable to pay up. Copies of the maps, which are extremely detailed, will be held at the CRO, and they are accompanied by a list (the apportionment) of the names of all owners and occupiers of land and cottages.

Armed with your maps and all the information you can glean from local histories and guides, it's time to go and walk the paths your ancestors trod. Only on foot can you get an idea of how much time a day they spent walking from one point to another – to the farm, to the school, to the well, to the shop. Can you find the actual cottage where they lived? This may prove more difficult as street names, house numbers and so on may have changed over the years, but with intelligent use of addresses taken from certificates, the census, directories and other sources, and with a knowledge of local history, you may be able to track it down. One place you will certainly want to visit is the churchyard or cemetery where your ancestors lie.

Churchyards and cemeteries

Monumental inscriptions on gravestones, and memorials inside churches can be very useful sources of information about ages, relationships, addresses and occupations, as well as the date of death. Family History Societies have worked on producing surveys and indexes of MIs in their county; see their websites or ask at the CRO.

The first cemetery in England was opened in 1825 and most counties have municipal burying grounds that date back to the middle of the 19th century. Their early registers are usually deposited at the CRO, and later ones can be consulted at cemetery offices.

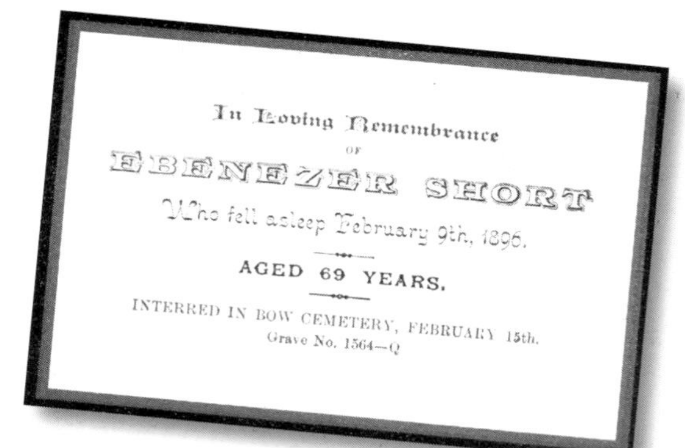

Memorial cards, sent to friends and acquaintances after a funeral, may give valuable information leading to the cemetery where the deceased was buried, and even the grave number.

Chapter 14
Moving About

People moved about the country with an ease that we might find surprising today. Young men and women left home and travelled miles away for their first job, perhaps living in as a servant. Men joined the army, even for a short while, and were posted anywhere in the U.K. or the Empire. Seasonal migration was an annual event, when men and women moved from parish to parish seeking the work that came with the regular turn of the agricultural year. At any point on their travels they might marry and settle down, sometimes hundreds of miles from where they were baptised.

While you may find the bulk of your research comes within the records of England and Wales, your ancestors could well have crossed into, or out of, Scotland or Ireland, or indeed migrated into or out of the U.K. It is not possible here to do more than mention some of the relevant sources, with more information available in the books and on the websites listed below, but do consider them. This is always a possible answer to 'missing' ancestors.

Scotland

Scottish records evolved separately from those for England and Wales and there are many differences in the documents and in the legal and social systems of the two countries that you will need to understand to make the most of your research. Civil registration, for instance, began there in 1855 and the certificates give more information than our own. They are kept at New Register House, Edinburgh EH1 3YT and it is possible to see the certificate itself rather than just the index entry. Census returns are similar to those for England. The probate system is different, though, as before 1823 probate was gained through secular courts called commissariots, while from 1824 the responsibility was transferred to civil sheriff courts.

The website of the National Archives of Scotland, www.nas.gov.uk, has information on civil registration, wills and the census. There is a

Scottish section for the IGI, and the LDS website, www.familysearch.org, includes this as well as the 1881 census free to view. However, the best way to get an overview of what resources are available is to visit www.scotlandspeople.gov.uk, which is the official government site of genealogical data for Scotland and includes in a searchable format the civil registration records, old parish registers, the census and Scottish wills 1513-1901.

Ireland

The situation is different in Ireland because it was administered by England until 1922, when Eire, the Republic of Ireland, was formed and the six remaining counties (Antrim, Armagh, Down, Fermanagh, Londonderry and Tyrone) were named Northern Ireland as part of the United Kingdom. Records are therefore divided between the two countries. Added problems arose when a fire destroyed many irreplaceable records in 1922, including almost all original probate documents, and when the 1861 to 1891 census returns were destroyed once the government statistics had been produced, making the 1901 census the first complete record that can be seen. In Ireland, general civil registration began in 1864 (with non-Catholic marriages registered since 1845).

There are several good guides to researching Irish ancestors (the difficulties mentioned above should not put you off; there are many indexes, abstracts and collections that can help you fill the gaps) and the websites of the government bodies have a great deal of useful information, with research leaflets available on all subjects; the Irish Genealogical Research Society is also helpful (www.igrsoc.org). The records for Northern Ireland were kept separately from 1st January 1922. The General Register Office of Northern Ireland is at Oxford House, 49-55 Chichester Street, Belfast BT1 4HL (www.groni.gov.uk); the Public Record Office of Northern Ireland is at 66 Balmoral Avenue, Belfast BT9 6NY (www.proni.gov.uk). The General Register Office of Ireland is at Joyce House, 11/13 Lombard Street East, Dublin 2 (www.groireland.ie); and the National Archives of Ireland is at Bishop Street, Dublin 8 (www.nationalarchives.ie).

Advertisements offering free land appeared in rural newspapers in the early 1900s, enticing farmers to emigrate to Canada.

The Rest of the World

Millions of people have emigrated over the past two centuries in the hope of finding a better future in a new land. You may discover that a branch of your family went to the United States, Australia, New Zealand, Canada, South Africa, or elsewhere in the old British Empire. There was also the forced emigration suffered by those who were transported to the colonies as a punishment, or who went out as indentured servants, little better than slaves.

On the other hand, perhaps your family originated outside this country. You may already know this, or it may come as a surprise. There can be very few families who do not have foreign origins on some branch of their tree.

Whether emigrant or immigrant, there are family history societies all over the world that will put you in touch with people with the same interests as yourself. Genealogy is a universal passion and the ease of communication that the Internet provides has opened up the world in a way that would have been impossible just a few years ago.

Finding out more

Tracing Your Scottish Ancestors, Simon Fowler, TNA, 2001

Scottish Family History on the Web: A Directory, Stuart A. Raymond, SoG, 2nd ed, 2004

Tracing Your Irish Ancestors, Simon Fowler, TNA, 2001

Irish Family History on the Web: A Directory, Stuart A. Raymond, FFHS, 2nd ed, 2004

Emigrants and Expats: A Guide to Sources on UK Emigration and Residents Overseas, R. Kershaw, TNA, 2002

Immigrants and Aliens: A Guide to Sources on UK Immigration and Citizenship, R. Kershaw & M. Pearsall, TNA, 2nd ed, 2004

Family History on the Move, R. Kershaw & M. Pearsall, TNA, 2006

Huguenot Ancestry, Noel Currer-Briggs & Royston Gambler, Phillimore, 2001

Tracing Your West Indian Ancestors, Guy Grannum, TNA, 2002

The Family and Local History Handbook, annual editions (current addresses for family history societies and record offices all over the world)

www.familyrecords.gov.uk/links.htm ('Immigration and Emigration' button)

www.genuki.org.uk/big/Emigration.html (links to many related sites). Genuki also has many links to sites useful for researching Scottish and Irish ancestors.

Chapter 15

Sharing your Research

Family history is a hobby for a lifetime. You may never neatly end your research. There will always be a date that eludes you, an ancestor who remains a stubborn mystery, a family whose origins seem to stretch no further back than the 1750s or so. That is part of the magic of this fascinating and frustrating obsession. And it is also the reason why you should not put off sharing your research until you are 'finished'.

Every so often, gather together all that you have uncovered so far and pass it on to the wider world. How you do that depends on your own interests and personality, but don't let your hard work flower unseen. There are probably people out there who can add to your tree, if they are given the chance to hear about it.

1. Once a year or so, at the very least, update family members with what you have uncovered so far. That way, the information is passed on in small, interesting chunks rather than in an undigestible mass.

2. Set up your own web page and publish your findings on the Internet.

3. Write up your family history so far. You can be as formal or as informal as you like - it is your project and you should produce something that pleases you. You might decide, for instance, to write about several generations, or perhaps just one individual who has intrigued you. Desktop publishing on your computer has opened up new horizons for authors whose books have a limited, local appeal.

4. Deposit your family tree at the Society of Genealogists, which has a huge collection of published and manuscript genealogies.

5. Give a talk based on your research, perhaps to a group from the local family history society. Alternatively, write an article for the society journal.

Whatever you decide, do justice to your hard work:

- Be honest.
- Be scrupulous in citing sources and authorities.
- Never use someone else's work without asking them, and give them full credit for it. You must be as aware of the laws of copyright, including work taken from the Internet, as any professional writer or researcher.
- Acknowledge any people who have helped you in any way.

Finding out more

Writing Up Your Family History, John Titford, Countryside Books, 2003

How to Write a Family History, Terrick V.H. Fitzhugh, Alpha Books, 1988

Appendix

Useful Addresses & Websites

The National Archives, Kew, Richmond, Surrey TW9 4DU
telephone: 020 8392 5271
www. nationalarchives.gov.uk
Formerly the Public Record Office, this is the place where the national archives of the United Kingdom and England are kept. There is a vast amount of material here for family historians. It is open to all to use. You just need to have a reader's ticket issued when you first arrive (no need to make an appointment, but make sure you have some form of identification with you).There are regular beginners' tours of the various reading rooms and it is worthwhile joining one, as it can be a bewildering experience at first. The staff are extremely helpful and used to advising newcomers, but try to go properly prepared by reading their excellent guides or looking at their website. The records available online are increasing all the time.

Family Records Centre,
1 Myddelton Street, Islington, London EC1R 1UW
telephone: 020 8392 5300
website: www.familyrecords.gov.uk
The GRO indexes to births, marriages and deaths since 1837 (and many other returns relating to those events overseas) are kept here, as well as the national census on microfilm, indexes to wills 1858-1943 and PCC wills to 1858, death duty registers, etc. There is also a link to the GRO ('Scots Link') for Scotland. At the time of writing there are plans to transfer many FRC records to TNA at Kew – check websites for up to date details.

Federation of Family History Societies,
PO Box 2425, Coventry CV5 6YX
www.ffhs.org.uk; www.genfair.com; www.familyhistoryonline.net
Find out where your nearest family history society is based, either for your

own county or for the places your family came from. Annual subscriptions are small and you will receive a regular journal and updates on projects and publications. The Federation website has a link to GENfair, the 'one-stop shop' for family history societies' publications and details of all member societies. The Federation also runs the Familyhistoryonline website, which has over 60 million records for England and Wales available to search for a very small fee, compiled by Family History Societies.

Society of Genealogists,
14 Charterhouse Buildings, Goswell Road, London EC1M 7BA
telephone: 020 7251 8799
website: www.sog.org.uk
The Society has a copies of parish registers, transcripts and indexes, published and manuscript genealogies. You can join the Society (which entitles you to some free access to the pay-per-view records site www.originsnetwork.com), or use the library as a day visitor.

Institute of Heraldic & Genealogical Studies,
79-82 Northgate, Canterbury, Kent CT1 1BA
telephone: 01227 462618
website: www.ihgs.ac.uk
As well as having a prestigious library of genealogical resources, the IHGS runs courses in family history, including for the award of a Diploma and Higher Certificate in Genealogy.

British Library Newspaper Library,
Colindale Avenue, London NW9 5HE
telephone: 020 7412 7353
website: www.bl.uk/collections/newspapers.html
The Library holds the national archive of British and overseas newspapers, and of many magazines and journals. It is open to anyone over 18 years of age (take with you a form of identification bearing your signature). Their catalogue is on their website; a search on, for instance a county or town name is an excellent way to find out what newspapers were current for the period you are interested in.

Church of Jesus Christ of Latter-day Saints (LDS or Mormons)
www.familysearch.org
The LDS runs Family History Centres throughout the UK which are open to anyone to use. You can order films of parish registers, census returns and a great variety of other material to view at your local Centre, at a minimal cost. A full list of the Centres is on their website, and in the latest edition of the *Family and Local History Handbook* (see below). On FamilySearch, you can access the 1881 census, the IGI and other sources, completely free.

Gateways and Search Engines

The two most useful for beginners are:

www.genuki.org.uk
www.cyndislist.com

There are literally thousands of family history links from these two sites alone, although Cyndi's List has a bias towards American sources. More are listed in *Family History on the Web* (see below).

GENERAL FAMILY HISTORY BOOKS AND MAGAZINES

There is a great variety of 'How to' family history books on the bookshelves, of which this is merely a selection:
Ancestral Trails, Mark Herber, Sutton Publishing, 2nd ed, 2004
Tracing Your Family Tree, Jean Cole & John Titford, Countryside Books, 4th ed, 2003
Journeys in Family History: The National Archives' Guide to Exploring Your Past, David Hey, TNA, 2004
Tracing Your 19th Century Family History, Stuart A. Raymond, FFHS, 2005
Tracing Your 20th Century Family History, Stuart A. Raymond, FFHS, 2003
The Genealogist's Internet, Peter Christian, TNA, 3rd ed, 2005
Family History on the Web: An Internet Directory for England & Wales, Stuart A. Raymond, FFHS, 2004/5 (regularly updated)
Tracing Your Ancestors in The National Archives: The Website and Beyond, Amanda Bevan, TNA, 7th ed, 2006

Published each year by Robert Blatchford Publishing (33 Nursery Road, Nether Poppleton, York YO26 6NN), *The Family and Local History Handbook* (10th ed, 2006) contains every address you will ever need to know, plus articles on aspects of family history. Website: www.genealogical.co.uk.

There are several family history magazines on sale, which are excellent for keeping up to date with what is being published and for general aspects of genealogy, including:

Family Tree Magazine
Practical Family History
Family History Monthly
Ancestors (the magazine of The National Archives, available by subscription)

GENEALOGY SUPPLIERS

There are many commercial suppliers of genealogy reference materials, books, etc, including:
S&N Genealogy, West Wing, Manor Farm, Chilmark, Salisbury SP3 5AF; tel: 01722 716121; website: www.GenealogySupplies.com
Archive CD Books, 5 Commercial Street, Cinderford, Glos, GL14 2RP; tel: 01594 829870; website: www.archivecdbooks.org
Stepping Stones, PO Box 295, York YO32 9WQ; tel: 01904 400503; website: www.stepping-stones.co.uk

Index